Things They Fail to Tell You During Pregnancy

A QUICK GUIDE AND INSIGHT

Ashley Shayne Pierce

Copyright © 2018 Ashley Shayne Pierce

All rights reserved. In accordance with U.S. Copyright Act of 1976, the scanning, uploading, and electronic sharing of any part of this book without permission of the publisher constitute unlawful piracy and theft of the author's intellectual property. No part of this book may be reproduced in any form by any electronic or mechanical means (including photocopying, recording or information storage and retrieval) without permission in writing from the author or publisher. Thank you for your support of the author's rights. For bulk wholesale copies please contact the publisher at richterpublishing@icloud.com.

Published by Richter Publishing LLC www.richterpublishing.com

Book Cover Design: Photo credit RTF123

Editors: Natalie Meyer & Monica San Nicholas

Proofreader: Nastassia Clarke

ISBN: 9781945812354

ISBN-13: 978-1-945812-35-4

DISCLAIMER

This book is designed to provide information on pregnancy only. This information is provided and sold with the knowledge that the publisher and author do not offer any legal or medical advice. In the case of a need for any such expertise consult with the appropriate professional. This book does not contain all information available on the subject. This book has not been created to be specific to any individual people or organization's situation or needs. Reasonable efforts have been made to make this book as accurate as possible. However, there may be typographical and or content errors. Therefore, this book should serve only as a general guide. This book contains information that might be dated or erroneous and is intended only to educate and entertain. The author and publisher shall have no liability or responsibility to any person or entity regarding any loss or damage incurred, or alleged to have incurred, directly or indirectly, by the information contained in this book or as a result of anyone acting or failing to act upon the information in this book. You hereby agree never to sue and to hold the author and publisher harmless from any and all claims arising out of the information contained in this book. You hereby agree to be bound by this disclaimer, covenant not to sue and release. You may return this book within the guarantee time period for a full refund. In the interest of full disclosure, this book contains affiliate links that might pay the author or publisher a commission upon any purchase from the company. While the author and publisher take no responsibility for any virus or technical issues that could be caused by such links, the business practices of these companies and or the performance of any product or service, the author or publisher has used the product or service and makes a recommendation in good faith based on that experience. All characters appearing in this work have given permission. Any resemblance to other real persons, living or dead, is purely coincidental. The opinions and stories in this book are the views of the author and not that of the publisher. Product photos are from Amazon, Target or Walmart. Other photos are from RTF123.com

Dedication

I would like to dedicate this book to many people who have helped me along the way:

To my cousin Brandy, who gave me the idea to write this book.

To my husband Andrew and his parents, Robert and Shirlene, who watched our son, listened to my banter about the book, and kept encouraging me to finish.

To my friend Christine, who would give me input through her different experiences.

To What's Up Moms, for giving me inspiration.

Lastly, to anyone who listened to me, gave me ideas, encouraged me, and supported me through this time.

Contents

Chapter 1 Before Pregnancy 1

Chapter 2 The 1st Trimester, Weeks 1-12 11

Chapter 3 The 2nd Trimester, Weeks 13-26 18

Chapter 4 The 3rd Trimester, Weeks 27-40 26

Chapter 5 Postpartum 33

Chapter 6 My Ultimate Lists and Must Haves 44

Chapter 7 How to Save 66

Chapter 8 DIY (Do It Yourself) 74

Chapter 9 Man's Survival Guide 81

Chapter 10 Mom Life 90

Summary/Final Thoughts 99

About the Author 102

Acknowledgements

I would like to acknowledge:

My friends and family, for encouraging me to continue writing.

What's Up Moms, for always being such an inspiration.

Richter Publishing, for making my dreams of being an author come true.

Introduction

There are many questions prospective parents have when planning to become pregnant or while currently pregnant, especially if this is a first-time pregnancy. Often, the first question is "Can I afford this?" The response from everyone will generally be that there is never a "right time" to have kids, and affording them will always be difficult. I believe you can do anything with knowledge, resources, and support. This book will discuss everything from pre-pregnancy to postpartum, with insight on financial and insurance aspects and a look into what postpartum is really like. These are the subjects they fail to mention in other books and what we learn from either from word-of-mouth or personal experience.

Chapter 1
Before Pregnancy

    First, if you are consciously trying to get pregnant, it's always important to make sure you want to for the right reasons. During a rough patch, many couples think that a baby can bond them or make them closer together after the birth. This can make you feel closer at the time, but unless the complication is resolved, it hasn't gone away—it's just been delayed. For this reason, it's best to be sure you are in a healthy relationship and not having a child due to fear or because you feel there's an expectation.

    If you want to start a new career, begin that process *before* pregnancy. There is definitely the option for you to go back to school after kids, just know that it's not an easy walk in the park. Parents who go back to school after having children, no matter the age, need to be prepared for the sacrifices not only you make, but the rest of the family including children will make during school. Some parents can live and transition well, while others give up because they feel that the sacrifices are too much on their personal and family life. What helped me finish school before children was reminding myself that it would provide my child a better life, because with the use of my education, we wouldn't have to live paycheck to paycheck. Remind yourself that school is temporary and will eventually end with a graduation and diploma in your hand.

Before you embark on parenthood, have that one last vacation as a couple. This might be the last time you vacation alone for a very long time without worrying about anyone not with you. Make your last vacation worth it and be selfish and guilt-free for the last time.

Now that you're in a healthy relationship, it's time to move on to location and place. Are you in the location you want to be or do you want to move? Is this a location where you want to settle? Consider what is important to you and your partner, whether it's schools, a big city for transportation, after-school resources, or closer/further from family. Next, is your place big enough for a new addition to the family? A baby will grow from an infant through their childhood and will need their own room. Babies require space for all their things, from cribs to clothes and toys. Be prepared to be overwhelmed by the gifts from friends, family, co-workers and loved ones that will need to be stored in the baby's room. The longer you wait to move during your pregnancy, the more difficult the strain you will be putting onto your body. If you move during the last trimester, you can expect fatigue, lower extremity swelling, back pain, and pelvic pain/pressure, not to mention stress and anxiety from not having this task accomplished yet. The best advice I can offer is to move as soon as you can or just plan on getting pregnant after the move, if at all possible. Have realistic expectations for your move, including cost, commute to places you frequent, whether you should buy or rent your home, and whether the style of home suits your family's lifestyle. Make sure you can still afford to live there with reduced income during maternity leave.

Having and raising a baby will be a big expense in your life. If possible, pay off as much debt as you can (like credit cards and loans), and know that you *will* need to use a credit card during maternity leave. Make sure you and your partner both have means of transportation. If you live in a big city with wonderful public transportation, utilize options such as buses and trains that don't require a car seat. If this doesn't apply to you and you require your own personal vehicle, try to have access to your own. Sharing a car can make things like appointments harder to keep considering multiple schedules. Have your vehicle serviced and running great with working air conditioning and heat, as babies aren't able to regulate their body temperature for a while and temperature control in the car will help. Having tune-ups and oil changes can help keep your vehicle in good shape and prevent being stranded on the side of the road. Always have a backup plan if you break down, because that does happen. Car insurance provides some protection, and you can add a supplemental roadside service, like AAA.

Most importantly, you need to make sure that you're taking care of yourself. Make your necessary doctor's appointments, tell them you are planning on getting pregnant, and ask if they have any advice. Your gynecologist will more than likely recommend starting prenatal vitamins before conception, weight loss if applicable, eating healthy, reducing stress, and increasing water intake. Begin a workout routine, even if it's just walking. Light exercise is better than nothing and can help out later on during the labor process. Keep in mind for the next 40 weeks, your body is not the only one you're nourishing. Remember that what you eat, drink, inhale, and do to your body will affect baby's growth and development. Your actions can have serious and even catastrophic consequences.

Before becoming pregnant, look into and obtain medical insurance and short-term and/or long-term disability either through your job or your partner's job, the marketplace and/or government programs (Tricare, Medicaid, etc.). When choosing medical insurance, look at what the policy covers, the copay (amount paid for each doctor visit), and the deductible (amount paid before the insurance will cover either everything, or a specified percentage). You will begin to pay this upon your first appointment at eight weeks, and normally this is paid off by the time you are five months pregnant. Also consider that it's cheaper to be pregnant through the year, since insurance rolls over every January. If you get pregnant and pay within the fiscal year, you only pay up to your deductible and not a penny more. If you already have seen the end of the previous year and will deliver into the next year, you still pay for appointments that will continue to go toward your deductible. Remember, deductibles are set by the insurance company and can vary in amount. If you are unsure about of the amount or out-of-pocket maximum, call your human resources department and ask them to explain it to you before you accept the policy if you're starting a new job. If you already have the policy, call the insurance company and ask what payment will be expected of you for you to have a baby.

Many consumers do not realize that the amount you pay not only varies by which insurance plan you have, but also by who the primary card holder is. If you are listed as a dependent under another individual's insurance, your deductible is twice as much as the primary card holder. When choosing a plan, consider which care providers are in-network vs. out-of-network (in-network will be cheaper and may have a special rate for policyholders with your insurance company), and check to see which hospital they have privileges in to deliver your baby. This becomes important when choosing a pediatrician. You can always call customer service with your insurance company to ask a representative these questions or look it up on their website. You can request a list of CPT codes from your gynecologist's office that they will use to bill throughout your pregnancy. Current Procedural Technology (CPT) codes consist of medical codes used to report and bill services provided to the patient. Call your insurance provider to make sure your insurance covers the services provided from the CPT codes in order to prevent any surprise out-of-pocket expenses. Some insurance companies will require a preauthorization two weeks before a procedure and/or test. Sometimes physicians don't pay attention to this and will bill it without prior authorization, resulting in you paying an out-of-pocket expense.

The next item to consider is short-term and long-term disability. This type of coverage should be purchased through either your work company or directly through another insurance company. Short term is often used if the person is having surgery or is pregnant and will be out-of-commission for up to 12 weeks; long-term is used for anything that goes beyond twelve weeks. It has come to my attention that some companies only provide one or both insurance(s), so if you're planning on becoming pregnant, see what benefits your company offers. Many people only get short-term disability since the Family Medical Leave Act (FMLA) only covers up to 12 weeks. Short-term disability pays in one lump sum, and you will be paid 40 to 60 percent of your gross pay. The difference between gross and net pay is that gross pay is calculated before taxes and insurance are deducted, and net pay is the final amount after deductions. Also, keep in mind you only sign up for insurance when you are a new hire or during annual enrollment (normally around October). If possible, wait to become pregnant until this is complete, or you may not be covered. To receive FMLA benefits during maternity leave, you must be with the company for at least a year, so you will have to plan that out as well.

Before you get your disability check, your company will require you to use up any PTO/PDO (paid time off/paid days off) and sick pay for the first two weeks, then the insurance company will be notified by human resources. From then, it will take an additional two weeks until you receive your check. You can be your own advocate and keep in contact by email with human resources to notify when you will begin your leave. You may have to contact the insurance company providing your disability check to keep the ball rolling.

If you consider yourself a regular person (and by that I mean not a celebrity or person that makes so much money you don't have to clip coupons or look at sales), start saving money early using coupons for diapers, wipes, and formula and just stock up. It can be difficult to get a big box of formula when you don't have any steady income, because without coupons or deals, that can cost you from $20 to $40 dollars easily. If you go on big formula web sites (Enfamil, Similiac), they send free samples for newborns. Start stocking on everything; it's okay if your baby outgrows an unopened box of diapers from your stockpile. If you return the box for store credit, you can use it later to buy the new size you need. You can start looking at sales trends and compare what's cheaper using online digital coupons, the Target Cartwheel app, Target REDcard, and store and manufacturer coupons. Don't forget that some stores price match or take competitor coupons; it doesn't hurt your wallet to ask. Another big way to save money is to buy gently used items from friends, thrift stores, yard sales in your area, and even eBay to cut down on baby costs.

I can't stress enough how often I have heard from first-time moms how they want to exclusively breastfeed. This is a wonderful idea, but that doesn't mean you shouldn't have a backup plan. If nothing else, you can sell any unused cans of formula. Sometimes people forget that when/if they return to work, it can be hard to pump as often as you need to. Another reason to consider this is your body. No matter what level of fitness you've tried to maintain, you likely won't produce enough of what your baby needs and you'll require supplementation. Lastly, and I can personally attest to this, being involved in an accident or getting sick can require you to take pain medications or other medicines that are harmful to the baby. I had definitely not *planned* to get into a car accident and to need surgery. I had to switch to formula only, compared to pumping what I could with a busy and demanding schedule and using formula as a supplement. Just be prepared and at least have some stock. This doesn't make you a bad mom, it just provides a safety net for your kid to receive nutrition Instead of going hungry.

If you haven't found the medical practice group you want to deliver your baby, ask around and see who your friends and family have used. Be sure to find out where they have privileges as well, because you may not like the hospital they're affiliated with. Sometimes the same company but different locations deliver at different hospitals. Make sure you like all the doctors there and feel comfortable that any one of them might deliver your baby. I've had friends say, "I like everyone but one doctor." It always seems that the disliked doctor ends up being the one to deliver, and remember, they also do your postpartum visit.

It's important to train your pets to get used to the disruption from the new family member. You and your pets must make this adjustment of a baby screaming frequently day and night. Make sure your pet is friendly around children, and consider whether professional training is necessary, or if it seems that a smooth transition is impossible, perhaps consider rehoming the pet to a better fit. The more time you spend on training, the easier the adjustment can be.

To the ladies who want to be moms but there is no husband or man in their life: it has seemed in this generation that if you focus on your career, it's harder to find a partner. And now that your clock is ticking, you're afraid of time running out. If you choose this path, whether by adoption, artificial insemination, or the old-fashioned way, make sure you know what you're getting yourself into. It's not easy or glamorous being a single mom, so make sure you have support. This can be a lonely road sometimes, and it might be harder to date once a child is in the picture. Decide on what you really want, what's important for you to have, and really be honest with yourself.

Lastly, open your ears and listen to people who have already gone through this process. You will continually hear how they could have done something differently, whether by stocking up on supplies or restricting visitors. Just because they suggest something doesn't mean you need to do it, but you'll at least get some expectations and suggestions from their experience. Take what you hear and apply it to your life. Besides, do you really want to repeat the mistakes they've already made, now that you don't have to "live and learn" from them yourself?

ASHLEY SHAYNE PIERCE

Chapter 2
The 1st Trimester, Weeks 1 - 12

    First things first: share the great news that you will be a parent. Everyone is different and that's perfectly fine. Share how you want, with whoever you want, once you and your partner are ready. You can tell just future grandma and grandpa, or the soon-to-be aunt and uncle, or you can tell your closest friend first. Just know that it's up to you; this is *your* happy news. Do it when you feel comfortable, and don't let anyone pressure you. For tips on fun ways to share the news, there are always great websites like Pinterest to help you make it memorable. I found out I was pregnant on Christmas Eve, and I placed my home pregnancy test (EPT stick) in a card and presented it to both his parents and mine. I've also seen an ultrasound posted on social media, stating "Another guest will be joining this Thanksgiving." My favorite was three pairs of shoes together, where it looks like a math problem hinting that mom and dad will soon be three.

I was confused by what the doctors would use as the date of conception. I knew my exact date, but medical professionals will go by the day of your last period. This is very important to know in order to give an accurate due date and plan your future doctor's appointments. Before setting up your first appointment at eight weeks gestation, you must pick an office. Remember to consider whether the office is in-network with your insurance company to save money, whether you like the office, and whether you like the doctor and hospital where you'll deliver. After you find your office it's time to make your eight-week appointment.

Your eight-week appointment is a milestone because a lot happens. At this point, you'll receive a contract agreement of payment. This will include your deductible, then how much your monthly payments are with the total cost of service that insurance will pay after you've met the deductible. This is also when you confirm the pregnancy by ultrasound. Please note that this ultrasound is transvaginal. The technician will insert a wand into your vagina, which requires you to be naked from the waist down. After this ultrasound, the rest will be done over your abdomen. From this appointment on, you will have to pee in a cup to track the protein in your urine, so always come with a full bladder or a big water bottle in hand. Sometimes the ultrasound technician can see your baby better on the screen when you have a full bladder, so ask before you leave your sample.

Before you leave your appointment, ask the front desk for the list of CPT codes mentioned in Chapter 1, because you can later call your insurance company to confirm that they cover all tests and procedures billed to you. Sometimes before an insurance company will cover a procedure, they require prior authorization from a doctor. Set up your next appointments and know that it's policy to rotate and see every doctor before you deliver. Sometimes this is scary for women, especially if they've never had a male doctor before and have to see one in this process. Take a deep breath and relax. They have the same goal as you—for you to deliver a healthy baby.

After your appointment, call your insurance provider about the CPT codes, and ask whether they have a healthy pregnancy program. The healthy pregnancy program will provide you with a choice pregnancy books, such as one from Mayo Clinic. It also provides you an on-call nurse who calls to ask how're you doing and who you can call any time you have a question. Lastly, they provide local resources for free baby classes, and many insurance companies supply free breast pumps toward the end of pregnancy, which you can ask about. Find out when you can obtain the pump and where they recommend you get it. The pump covered by your insurance can normally be ordered 30 days before your due date, and it will require a prescription from your doctor. Take note of who the insurance company suggests you order from; they'll often suggest medical supply companies like McKesson. In my case, I had to send an email to the company providing the script, as I had initially talked to someone over the phone. You can only obtain your pump 30 days before your due date. Do this as soon as you hit your 30 days till delivery to give the company time to ship it to you. This is a great free option if you have insurance, otherwise there are always people selling theirs if your insurance doesn't provide this option and you find them a bit expensive to buy new.

Some of my girlfriends and I enjoyed using baby apps while we were pregnant. They helped connect our partners to the baby and gave new information every week going over the baby's development and what mom could expect. There are many apps out there to choose from, and I preferred Ovia of the ones I tried. I liked that it was easy to use and the maker had a parenting app and an ovulation app as well. I loved that you could put down milestones and appointment dates, as well as log blood pressure and weight. Some doctors' offices also provide apps that can be useful. The apps will tell you when your next appointment is and with whom, and have trackers for weight, blood pressure, blood sugar, and contractions. I recorded everything that was applicable. If you do this, it can gave the doctors insight at your appointments, since you rotate doctors.

The eight week sonogram confirms the pregnancy, making this real and confirming, "I'm really having a baby!" I already mentioned the first sonogram was transvaginal. What a lot of sources fail to mention about the 12-week appointment is the pressure the sonographer will place over your belly when you have a full bladder. Mine wanted me to wait to pee to see the baby better. That technician will be looking everywhere for the baby in there, and some babies are more cooperative than others. They might even bounce or it might feel like light jabs on your belly to move the baby around; no worries, this is normal.

My best advice for all new moms is to ask exactly what is on your mind, even if you think it's a dumb question. Chances are, they've heard it all before. The staff are all professional and are there to answer questions. Besides, we don't come equipped with this knowledge, and they've studied labor and delivery and can give great knowledge, insight, and resources, pointing you in the right direction. Some patients fail to give a full medical history in their first appointment, but the doctors ask to better serve you, so it's better to be forthcoming. If you have a history of you or your family having problems, your health can be monitored more closely, which isn't a bad thing. I came in with no medical problems besides asthma; however, my family has a history of mental and psychological issues and autism. It's better to know too much than not enough. Don't be ashamed or embarrassed that you or your family are not "in perfect health." Who cares? Your mission is to deliver a happy and healthy baby. Hiding these issues won't help you or your baby. So, be open and honest and ask tons of questions until you understand what's being said. If it helps, I had a notebook to write questions and answers down with a folder I brought to every appointment to keep myself organized, including payment receipts.

You might not have a clue about names yet, but by the next trimester, you can know the gender if you want, and can start brainstorming. You and your partner might not agree on a name as easily as you thought. Or, some couples don't want to name the baby until they meet the little one. Personally, I'm a planner and wanted to monogram blankets and other items. Don't let this process stress you out. It was fun seeing the styles of names my husband and I liked or disliked. They may even surprise you in a funny way. There are many ways to look up names and meanings, but when you do decide on a name, make sure you really like it and are not just trying to make the other person happy. The kid will have this name for the rest of their life.

Lastly, don't base your pregnancy on everyone else you know. Every pregnancy is different. Even if you have multiple children, I can guarantee you that each will not be a carbon copy of the last one. Also, you can't put all your money on these old wives' tales, because if they were right, I should have had a girl, but I had a boy. Sometimes I think things like this make the mom have tunnel vision and then when you find out the gender, you might be disappointed. Just enjoy carrying that bundle of joy. If you are just having fun with the tales to pass the time, then go for it, but please don't let it upset you because your baby might just surprise you in ways you cannot explain.

THINGS THEY FAIL TO TELL YOU DURING PREGNANCY

Chapter 3
The 2nd Trimester, Weeks 13 - 26

First, we will discuss the sonograms because you normally only get a limited number of them depending on insurance and how high of a risk you are during your pregnancy. You can pay extra to find out baby's gender at 16 weeks, or just be patient and wait for the 20-week anatomy scan to find out. If you choose to wait, the 3D/4D sonogram—whichever is offered to you around 23 weeks—will be the last time you get a glimpse of baby until you deliver during a typical pregnancy. My family paid for the 4D ultrasound, but my friend became high risk and baby didn't cooperate with the anatomy scan and had several more sonograms than I did. So, my baby was easy to see for the technician while my friend's baby hid in the womb. It's anyone's guess if the baby will cooperate, you can never know until you're in the hot seat.

After you find out the gender (if you choose to), you can have a gender reveal party, go registry scanning, and finalize names. These are all fun and memorable things you can do with your partner. Doing these things together helps get them involved, and getting involved sooner rather than later when you are up late doing a diaper change is preferable. There are so many unique options to try for a gender reveal party from cake, balloons, revealing paint that's on your belly, and colored powder. The possibilities are endless. Like with your pregnancy reveal, Pinterest will of course be a great resource to check out for creative gender reveal ideas. Just remember to have fun sharing the news.

One of my favorite things was going to different stores to register for baby shower gifts. Around sixteen to twenty weeks is a good time to plan on doing this. I did several registries for different reasons: Walmart is everywhere, has cheap prices, and can ship from online; Target has great sales along with Cartwheel for savings and the REDcard gives you 5% off in store and online and free shipping; Amazon for those who cannot live without their Prime membership; and lastly Babies "R" Us for the variety of things the other places didn't have with tons of options on big necessary items. This part is fun but can also be overwhelming the first time. Some of these places also give you a freebie bag full of baby goodies. I had never seen so many travel systems and car seats before. Let others guide you to products they loved and avoid the products they hated. I will include a list of my personal must haves in another chapter. I also asked the sales people what sold well and what was rarely returned. I figured if they didn't return it they must have loved it. If you are tight on cash for these large expenses, a later chapter will be focused on how to get some of these things cheaply or free.

Lastly, if you can and if you want to start finalizing names for baby if you plan on having anything monogrammed. If you choose to keep it a secret or have no clue and want to wait to see your child, then stick to your guns and don't let people pressure you to do anything you don't want to do. Have fun and be creative if you want.

While you are still mobile and not waddling yet go to a Prego Expo. They are fun, you get to window shop or buy items there, and best of all have a chance to win a door prize. The Prego Expo has a Facebook page to see when and where they will be. The Expo provides local vendors with tables with things to purchase and freebies. At the end of the maternity fashion show, they start raffling off featured items. What's there to lose by going, it's a good time and you can even score other freebies given out, including formula!

It's time to pick out a nursery theme and get it done before you fatigue too quickly to finish before the baby arrives. Let's face it, the nursery is about what you like. This may be your only chance to decorate the room as cute as you want. Before you know it, the kid will have an opinion of their own so you might as well enjoy it while it lasts. If you are waiting to find out gender for a surprise during delivery, going gender neutral is always safe with something like Winnie the Pooh or even Mickey Mouse. Also know it's ok to not decorate if you don't want to or if you are in an apartment and are limited on what you can do.

This is also the last time you can fly before having baby, so if you want a last-minute vacation that involves a plane you might want to do it now. However, don't forget how pregnant you are and how much walking or activity this vacation will entail. I went to New York City and was miserable walking as much as I did and regretted not taking as many taxis as I probably should have. My blistered feet and my sore back/pelvis did not thank me later for these decisions. Just keep in mind what your body will and will not allow you to do and stop before you have any type of discomfort. Rest and takes naps as necessary. If anyone gives you a hard time pull out the pregnancy card and remind them it's a hard job growing another human being inside of you. The best time to take a trip, from personal experience, is the end of the first trimester when you are cleared to go, especially if you are planning on flying or going places that require a lot of walking. My best suggestion is go sooner the better. When you have a baby, things will never be the same as they were before.

You might not want to think about this next topic, and can be a hot issue for new moms, but it must be discussed: child care. Be honest and realistic with your partner and yourself. There are several options: stay at home mom/dad, paying an in-house sitter, family/nonfamily members, and daycare. You must do what is right for your family and there are pros and cons for all sides. Just remember that you are not a bad parent with whatever you choose to do. All that matters is the baby is taken care of and someone works to get the bills paid so there is a roof over your heads and the lights are on. The sooner you decide the sooner you can save for which option you choose. Also keep in mind that if you go the daycare route, you need to check it out, get tips on which ones your friends like to send their kids to, if the one you want is affordable, and lastly to be put on the list so you can have a smooth transition when you return to work. Some daycares have long waiting lists so find out now rather than later.

Now about mom, your body is starting to change. This is when you need to invest in larger bras, underwear, clothes (maternity clothing to be exact), slip-on shoes (also house shoes/slippers), maternity belt (belly band), a reacher (hand grabber), and a good maternity pillow. Sleeping is just as important as wearing clothes that fit. The more well rested you are, the better your day will go, trust me. The further along you are, the harder it is to find a comfortable spot to sleep, so invest in this early on. I invested in a wedge pillow. It helped with my swollen feet, and when I could no longer sleep on my side and slept on my back, it helped with acid reflux as well. Having clothes that fit can go along way with self-image and esteem, as it's hard having your body and hormones change so much. I will also mention in a later chapter where and how to buy cheap affordable clothes. The belly band holds up your growing and heavy bump. I carried low and needed it, whereas a friend of mine carried higher and was fine. My must haves were slip-on sneaker/tennis shoes and house shoes/slippers. This helps you be able to put your shoes on by yourself and allows extra room when your feet swell. Toward the very end, I was so swollen I could only wear house shoes and couldn't even get on my sneakers. A reacher is considered adaptive equipment. You can see it used in therapy, but when you are round and short of breath and can't bend to the floor, let the reacher pick things up for you. If you are having problems putting on socks and shoes and taking them off, invest in the reacher along with a shoe horn and sock aide. YouTube will teach you how to use it to put on your socks without breaking a sweat.

Continue to communicate with your doctor even if your pregnancy seems normal and typical. There is no such thing as too much to share in the medical field. This is also the time in the pregnancy when you literally forget everything. When you hear about "pregnancy brain" it is no joke. I utilized calendars (digital and paper), note pads (digital and paper), and an app on my phone (Ovia Pregnancy) to put in milestones, what I ate, and how I was feeling. Even though you will forget everything from this point on, your pregnancy symptoms should be clearing up if you had any, but some never end. I had a cousin that couldn't hold anything down, needed to get IV fluids because of dehydration, and had low blood sugar throughout her pregnancy. I was fatigued, experienced swelling, and in the end experienced acid reflux. Each pregnancy will be different and never entirely the same.

While you still have the energy, this is the time to start budgeting and saving and determine how long of a leave you will be on. Most people take eight to twelve weeks or even an entire year off, but the time you take is completely up to you. You can put extra money in savings and what tons of people do during this time is also live off credit cards. During your last few months left of working you can build up on PTO/PDO (paid time off/paid days off) and sick pay. The first two weeks on maternity leave you will not get paid and companies will drain those accounts first. Stay in contact with HR (human resources) to let them know when you plan on taking your maternity leave. Some take a week before off from their due date and some will either wait until they go into labor or can no longer endure the work load due to pain/discomfort. Now is the time ask for the FMLA paperwork and short-term/long-term paperwork. Part of the paperwork must be filled out by your doctor and they charge around a $25 fee. When it comes to disability paperwork you will get 40-60% of your gross pay in one lump sum after the two weeks on maternity leave, and after you deliver your baby, the company will call your doctor's office to ask whether you delivered by cesarean section or vaginally. The more you keep in contact with HR letting them know when you went on leave and when you delivered your baby, the sooner they can get the ball rolling with the company you have disability insurance with to receive your money faster.

While you are making calls, you and your partner need to decide how you will obtain insurance for the baby. If you choose to add the baby to one of your current insurance plans, call up that insurance company and request the paperwork to add on the baby. You have 30 days to turn it in from the birth. I prefilled out paperwork, leaving spaces blank only if they needed to be completed post-birth, and this made it an easy transition for me without any hassle.

Lastly, sign up for freebies that send out coupons to the grocery store or discounted formula. The big formula companies will even send you out free samples. I know my grocery store has a Baby Club and they send me coupons for more than just baby items such as hand sanitizer, dairy, meat and much more. I applied to Enfamil and Similiac (why not both?) to get free newborn samples. Even you want to exclusively breastfeed, it's ok to have a backup plan. If you don't use your samples give them to a mom in need. Finally, start taking belly pictures. I have heard from moms who didn't that they regretted not taking any selfies.

THINGS THEY FAIL TO TELL YOU DURING PREGNANCY

Chapter 4
The 3rd Trimester, Weeks 27 - 40

Your pregnancy is coming to a close and can see the light at the end of the tunnel. This is when moms tend to "nest," which includes cleaning, decorating, and organizing. Some will go over the top in anticipation of the baby's arrival. You might as well use this energy to wash clothes and sterilize bottles. It's time to get serious and pick a pediatrician, or at least an office that you like. I knew who I wanted as a pediatrician, so I had no trouble there; for me, it was my coworker's wife. However, I wanted my husband to meet her first. Tons of facilities will allow you to schedule a pre-baby tour; this gives expecting parents a sense of whether they like the place or not. During the tour, you can meet with one or several doctors, and they will often give you a welcome bag with formula, coupons, and information on how to sign up to get free samples. If you have a hard time picking an office or doctor, ask around. People will let you know what they like and don't like. When the decision is made, make sure they accept your insurance, and ask to get the paperwork for the first visit. As with any appointment, allow yourself plenty of time to get there and be there prompt. They often expect you to be late.

Start looking through the packets your doctor can provide for you, take any birthing classes you are interested in, and do the hospital tour with your partner. You don't have to do all the suggested classes, but many are free through the healthy pregnancy program, if that's open to you. I only did a tour of the hospital and a class that goes through the stages of labor and discussed options for pain relief. My friend went to several classes (and had the time to do so), and she learned a lot. If you don't take a class, you'll either learn by word of mouth from friends, or the nurses at the hospital will teach you and provide demonstration.

During the last trimester, moms can feel overwhelmed, anxious, and stressed. Do what will reduce stress, whether it be paying off bills early, getting prenatal massage, getting paperwork together and filled out as much as possible, and making out an inventory of what else is needed for the baby. But before you make an inventory list, have a baby shower first if you have the means and interest for one. Make sure someone writes down a thorough list of gifts received, and send out thank-you notes before baby arrives, if you have the time and energy. After the shower, write out what it is you're still missing. If you can afford to get the items, then go for it, but if you're limited on funds, really think on whether the baby will need it or if it can wait until after you go back to work.

Get ready to decide on a birth plan. There are many things to consider: pain relief, natural or water birth, birthing center vs. hospital, and most importantly, who do you want as your support team? I had a friend who had just her husband and a doula. A doula is like a midwife and they can charge for services; however, my friend found a doula who was just finishing up with classes, so her service was free. I had my husband there and both of our moms. Most importantly, pick who you want there; who will make you feel comfortable and help you get past the finish line?

If you're expecting a boy, discuss with your doctor whether you plan on having your son circumcised. This is your choice; however, it's harder to clean during diaper changes. Boys are messy by nature, so it's easy for them to get an infection if the procedure is not done. I've changed a boy who was not circumcised, and it was weird for me since my son's had the procedure. I had to pull so much skin back to make sure it was cleaned well—and let's face it, you will have *many* diaper changes. Later, you'll need to teach them how to clean it properly themselves. Do yourself a huge favor and just have the procedure done for them; they won't remember it anyway.

If you're planning on breastfeeding, get the free breast pump provided through insurance if this is an option (see Chapter 2). My friend's insurance didn't provide the free pump, so she had to find an inexpensive option through online sales. I ordered mine exactly 30 days before my due date and got it in plenty of time before baby's arrival, so I could sterilize everything. I did wish that I'd gotten extra parts, such as extra pumping bottles, tubing, and tops that go onto the breasts. If you do choose to buy additional pieces to your pump, make sure the top of the bottle you'll use for pumping matches like the rest. Mine didn't, but I used it as an extra bottle for storing milk. When you're on-the-go and don't have a way to wash the parts before the next use, having extra until you can wash them at home is awesome.

We tend to forget that after you have the baby, it will be like having a constant period anywhere from six to eight weeks. I stocked up on big super pads, Depends (my favorite was Target brand), witch hazel, aloe, pain relief spray, stool softener pills, and Tylenol. I grabbed about three bags each of extra-large/long pads and Depends-type underwear. The hospital gives out mesh underwear, but I liked the coverage of Depends better because they didn't leak and get blood on my clothes. I wanted to make sure to also stock up on water that could be used for formula supplement and for myself, since I had planned to breastfeed. I found it to be cheaper to rent a water station for warm/cold water and purchase three five-gallon jugs through Nestle. This kept the cost under $20.

Now that you could deliver any day, install the car seat and put the baby diaper bag, your hospital bag, and some of your extra clothes in the car. This way, it will be less stress and hassle having everything just waiting in the car. This gives you peace of mind, and you'll freak out less if you have everything ready. You never know where you might be and if your water will break when you go into labor. I suggest having a complete set of extra clothes in the car in case your water breaks in public (shirts, underwear, pants, socks, shoes, towel to clean up with) because you just never know. I have heard that a majority of pregnant moms have the doctor break their water, but you never know which one you will be.

No shocker here, but toward the end, every mom is miserable. There is so much pelvic/lower back pain and pressure, that you are over being pregnant and want this baby to be out. At my last doctor's appointment, I had my membrane swept. They said this sometimes hurts, but I didn't feel pain. I just felt tons of pressure and was terrified I might pee on the doctor. The procedure is done in-office, and the doctor will put a hand in your vagina to sweep the membrane of your cervix. They will go about hand deep and this is similar when they check for dilation. There is a membrane around your cervix and they swear you will go into labor within a day or two. The process releases hormones that can induce labor. I had mine swept on a Tuesday afternoon and went into labor very early Wednesday morning. Another way to help baby to come out is by walking it out. You can be walking the baby out just before labor. When you are finally in active labor at the hospital, you can also continue to walk to help the progression with labor. I went to the mall to walk my baby out. My due date was in August, and as I was living in Central Florida, I felt like I was going to die in the heat and humidity. I found the best place for me to try to walk the baby out was at the mall. You may find this weird at first, but it has everything: food court, bathrooms, air conditioning, places to sit, and beds to lay on. I was looking at mattresses with my cousin one day at Macy's. When I had too much pelvic and back pain where I could only resolve this by lying down, I went to lay on my side on the mattress she was buying and felt better. Don't feel embarrassed to go and just lie down on a bed; people will have sympathy for you. No one ever said anything to me about it.

Lastly and most importantly, communicate anything and everything with your doctor. I cannot stress this enough! I mentioned anything, and every symptom, normal or not, and I'm glad I did. This is when you must listen to your body and be prepared for anything. I had an easy, typical pregnancy. I got to the hospital and I was three to four centimeters dilated and refused to go home. I was walking up and down the halls during contractions while I was in triage. The staff noticed how focused I was to get this baby out, and admitted me. They were glad they did because during labor, I developed HELLP syndrome, which is a serious, life-threatening condition. HELLP stands for hemolysis, elevated liver enzymes, low platelet count. What was worse was that I wasn't showing any symptoms of it and only found out I had it through my lab work. I had to get a blood transfusion, was put on a magnesium drip, and was given a 50% chance of surviving with my child. If I had not listened to my body and if the staff had sent me home, I could have died. I don't tell you this to scare you, but to show you how important it is to be open and completely honest with yourself and the hospital staff. Remember, everyone will have a different birth experience, but sometimes holding back can result in life or death in an instant. Therefore, you must be prepared for anything and trust your birthing team.

Chapter 5
Postpartum

Postpartum is when you are no longer pregnant, and the baby is now in your arms. You have been patiently waiting for this moment—once the baby comes out, they'll put it on your chest and that's normally when they start to sew you up. They also clean up the baby and do a few quick tests, all while sewing you up. Keep speaking up! Just because the baby is out doesn't mean you should stop communication. I had to keep telling the doctor I felt something sharp, and they had to numb me a few times. After I was sewn up, they had to take out my epidural (and FYI, if you're a bit on the hairy side, you may prefer to shave all that, because tape pulls, even around IVs). Yes, you will have an IV during your entire stay. My friend told me she didn't want Pitocin because her body would naturally make it. You don't have a say in this because this is protocol for hospital staff. This will help to speed up contractions, and let's face it, you don't want to be in labor forever. All I can say is, you will have an IV, and you'll have your vagina and cervix checked so much, you'll need to get over this pronto. Because of my situation with HELLP syndrome, I was bedbound for a few days and was made so weak from the magnesium drip, I couldn't move my limbs.

If you experience any problems or have any questions at all, please use your nurse button. You want to keep yourself and your baby healthy and safe, so ask for help. Why else did you come to the hospital? These are licensed, trained professionals; let them do their job. I called the CNA to take me to the bathroom the first time because I had no clue how to clean myself with stitches and pain down there. They were wonderful; I was afraid I would fall from weakness, and they taught me how to properly clean myself. I also had to call the nurse when I was weak from the magnesium drip to help me breastfeed my baby. The nurse literally had to lift my boob and put it in my baby's mouth. Modesty at this point is out the window.

Just because you are no longer in labor doesn't mean the constant visits are over with the nursing/hospital staff. There are several more tests to be done for both you and baby if you had any difficulties. You will have the pediatrician or their group members that will be there, and FYI, when you were in labor and even at your doctor's office visits, they ask who you want. If you continue to not name anyone, they'll use their own hospital staff. The nurse constantly does jaundice checks, the audiologist will come by, and the hospital photographer. My mother bought the thumb drive with the pictures; it was the best deal. If you plan on getting pictures there, I recommend bringing anything personalized or favorite outfits to have for baby's first photoshoot. I'm not saying their stuff isn't good, it is, but this is more personal.

While you're at the hospital, they provide diapers, cloths to use as wipes (I brought my own wipes), two long-sleeve shirts for baby to use as top/bottoms (again, brought my own), formula, mesh underwear, pads, Tucks (witch hazel pads to soothe stitches), pain relieving spray, and a water bottle to clean your vagina. I took everything they offered, and even asked for more pads, Tucks, and spray before I was discharged. Even though they supply some items, I brought some of my own, which will be listed in another chapter. Also pre-discharge, there are things that must be done before you walk/wheel out of there. When you are either in labor and delivery or up in your room, you must watch videos provided by the hospital that include information on breastfeeding, car seat safety, shaken baby syndrome, and caring for your newborn. Some videos are longer than others, and some are more interesting than others. Next, people will come into your room and pretty much quiz you about baby safety, especially when it comes to co-sleeping. They also educate heavily on postpartum depression. They want to make sure that your mental/emotional abilities are not impaired. Most importantly, before you leave the hospital, you will visit vital statistics to get your baby's birth certificate. In the Central Florida area in 2016, the price of a birth certificate was $14.

Now it is time to bring your baby home. The CNA will wheel you and baby down to the exit. I held my baby in the wheelchair. Don't forget you must have a car seat to take baby home—the hospital does not provide car seats. You will wait in the pull-up area while your ride home pulls up with the car. There are also usually carts available to help you bring down the items you brought with you for your stay. I was told that staff isn't supposed to do this, but we had help putting baby in his car seat since we were first time parents and a bit nervous. Let's face it, you are on your own from this point forward. You might get bombarded while you're at the hospital and you miss your own bed, but that 24/7 hospital staff safety net is no longer there once you return home.

Usually, family and friends are as ecstatic as you are for the new baby. If they offer help, take it; this will be a relief. I had people who wanted to help whether they were near or far, but had no clue how they could help. The best answer I had for them was meals. I had a girlfriend bring me a casserole, and my sister who lives in a different state gave my mom money to have her make me a fresh meal. You can always prep frozen meals or even a crockpot meal, because let's face it, cooking will not be a top priority. This takes away lots of stress and will give you plenty of time with the new baby. Also, having someone like a mom, sister, cousin, or an aunt stay with you isn't a bad idea. My mom stayed and helped with cooking and cleaning and it was very nice to just recover and enjoy the baby without freaking out over my house. My friend had a C-section and thankfully, her mom stayed with her for two weeks, because she needed to heal, couldn't drive, and was advised to not bend over. She would just have her mom or husband hand her the baby during feedings. So, whatever help is offered, just take it and say "thank you" with a smile.

Now that you're back home, it all becomes very real. The first night was terrifying for me. I was incredibly sore from the stitches, and I have a high bed, so I slept on the couch the first night, with the baby sleeping in his Rock 'n Play. After that night, I felt less terrified and slept in the bed with his Rock 'n Play nearby. I had him sleep in my room for two months and then moved him into his crib. Some friends did this longer than I did, which is fine. I knew I needed my space, and didn't want baby to get too used to co-sleeping. I do tend to need some space here and there, and your baby is either sleeping or you're holding them. Wanting a break from this doesn't make you a bad parent. To my friends who co-sleep and are now wanting this space back, and the child doesn't know how to self soothe and sleep on their own: this is your decision and there are so many opinions out there, all I can say is—do what makes you feel comfortable. To be honest, I didn't enjoy it when I first started the transition, but at six and nine months, I was glad I did.

It's time to get into a routine, except you have no idea what it is yet. You have no clue when or how often your baby will sleep/eat, and it keeps changing. Through this transition process, you will learn when it's best to make appointments for baby, when the baby will typically go down for naps/sleep, how much formula/breastmilk they eat, feeding positions, and what helps to soothe the baby. Speaking of routine, the whole being an adult thing still hasn't gone anywhere. You still need to pay the routine bills, and if you had health insurance through your work, you must send human resources a check to pay the bill to keep your insurance. I kept in contact with human resources before maternity leave by email discussing when and how much I needed to pay, including receiving/sending back my FMLA paperwork. If you have short-term disability, you'll get a lump sum anywhere from two to four weeks postpartum. I had emailed human resources giving them the date I delivered for short-term disability. Your short-term disability provider will also contact your doctor's office to verify you delivered your baby and whether it was a vaginal birth or C-section. Yes, it matters when it comes to recovery time.

After I was home for a while, I learned what helped relieve pain while sitting. Anything close to a round shape like a donut or a Boppy/maternity pillow works. It also took me a while to get into a comfortable position for breastfeeding. I even had a problem having the baby take to the left breast, but instantly latched to the right. Even with pumping, the left never produced as much as the right. I got to a point where the left would barely produce an ounce, where my right side would have up to six ounces. I would be so exhausted that I would just kept putting him on the easier side, but later I wished I would have kept trying. I would start to doze off during feedings at all hours. My husband was terrified and would make sure I was awake.

I noticed the baby was fussier at two weeks old and around a month old. What I mean is that when he woke up crying, it was like there was nothing I could do to console him. I tried to feed him, rock, sing, and play classical music. He just had to cry it out, but I never gave up, and I kept trying everything. You will eventually get into a rhythm and find what will work for you and baby. Even now, in order to sleep, my son requires his lovie, classical music, and his glowing sound-soothing seahorse.

Take tons of pictures. Most moms will do monthly pictures (which is easier to keep up with), but I have seen a few that do weekly shots in addition. Take pictures of precious moments and be in the present. These babies grow out of the newborn phase too quickly. Some moms (mainly with girls) will change their baby several times a day for pictures. I also enjoyed having a chalkboard to update on my son monthly. I saw some order boards already printed out through websites (Etsy, etc.), but this can become costly.

After you get into a better routine, you may want to get out of the house. Go have a date night with your partner; enjoy yourself and don't feel guilty about it. Another way to get out and see your friends/coworkers is to have a sip-and-see. A sip-and-see is hosted by a friend, and you can have wine, juice, snacks, appetizers, and go enjoy yourself, bring the baby, and basically pass the baby around to meet your friends. This is a nice way to catch up and know what's going on in the world beyond your house. Also, just being out of the house can help with or help prevent depression. When you have been home for so long, it's nice to have a change of scenery, to not be alone, and to start feeling normal again. When baby is a bit older (let's say around three months), you can do playdates and find free classes to attend (music, mommy and me, etc.). Not only are you getting out of the house, but you are meeting new moms like yourself, growing friendships, and building a network of support.

I found it very important to have mom friends, although you should always keep and make time for friends without children. It was nice to turn to the moms with more experience when I wasn't sure about something and wanted help or advice, and fun to be able to offer advice to moms with babies younger than mine. Sometimes one of us would be frustrated or scared on how much food they should give the baby. What brand of food? We would share websites, blogs, tips, and what worked and didn't work for our babies. This is a great support system to have; with it, you don't feel so alone. You can always ask the older women in your family, but it's nice to ask what works well now with today's modern technology.

Lastly, and the saddest topic, is returning to work. This is difficult for every new mom. Some moms will go back full-time, part-time, per diem, or stay at home. Plus, there is the issue on where your child will be, whether at home with a parent/family member/sitter, at a sitter's house, in-house daycare, or your standard daycare. I personally returned to work full-time, having my husband drop down to part-time on weekends, becoming a full-time stay-at-home dad. This worked out well for my family, but you must find what works best for you. I also wanted to go back to work full-time (I love what I do), and I make more money than my husband. We discussed this during the first trimester and after my husband did research, we found it was cheaper to have him stay home and work part-time than it would be to put the baby in daycare. Whatever you choose to do doesn't make you a bad parent. You still must go out in the world to make a living to support your family, and you're not a bad parent for doing so.

I have been seeing so much mom-shaming, and it's horrible. Moms are afraid that if they make a certain choice for their child, they will be shamed. I had a friend confide in me about the topic of homemade baby food vs. store-bought baby food. She was afraid she would be judged by family if she didn't make the food herself. I asked her if she knew anyone who cooked every night. She replied no. I reminded her that everyone has gone to the drive thru, ordered take out, or gone out to eat. You do this for special occasions, when you're on the go, too tired, or too busy dealing with life. So, do people not expect a mom with an infant who is significantly more tired than a single/married person with no children to also take a break? The main importance here is that you're feeding your child. Nobody handed out a manual on how to raise your baby. So, you get to raise and give your baby whatever you see fit, and that applies to your lifestyle. This even goes for breastfeeding. Some moms' bodies don't produce enough. In my case, I got hurt in a car accident and required emergency surgery. I was administered strong pain medication and went under anesthesia to fix my shattered kneecap. I knew before surgery I would not be able to continue breastfeeding. I would have to constantly pump and dump because of all the harmful things that could be given to the baby. This is why you always have a backup plan—in my diaper bag, I kept emergency supplement—because you never know what situation you may be put in. In the end, all that matters is that your baby is fed, clothed, diapered, and loved. Beyond this, mind your own business and keep your comments to yourself. You are not perfect, and no one else around is, either. Show support and help others.

Speaking of no longer breastfeeding, I had no clue how to stop. I was forced to stop due to my car accident. I had asked the emergency room nurse how to get my milk to dry up. I was told to get a tight sports bra and apply ice. I asked her if I could go between ice and heat and was told only ice, because heat helps with milk production. This took some time to work, and for a while I was still leaking, but I wasn't having any pain or soreness. I've also heard if you chose not to breastfeed from the get-go, there's a pill they can give you to stop your milk supply. If you take it immediately, you won't produce milk. If you had or attempted to nurse before taking this, it could take up to a week to dry up your milk. I'm not sure if they still offer this, but you can always ask.

Another hot topic regarding postpartum is having sex again. The doctor normally will say that in six to eight weeks, you can go back to regular sexual activity. I tried at six weeks and was still tight and sore, but felt better and more like myself after eight weeks. This can be different for everyone, so do what makes you comfortable. I also was terrified to even look where they stitched me up, and asked my husband if it looked healed.

Again, do what makes you feel comfortable, and don't let anyone pressure you. It's normal to fear having sex after such a traumatic experience on the body like childbirth.

Are you now wondering when you can get back into shape and get rid of that baby weight? For intense exercise, the doctor will tell you to wait around six to eight weeks after birth for internal recovery. Don't beat yourself up if you feel tired and drained from taking care of the baby and loss of sleep. I would sleep when the baby did, and not focus on exercise until I could get into a routine. Breastfeeding will wear you out physically, but it helps you lose weight a bit faster. There are several other ways to help lose weight, like workouts on the "What's Up Moms" YouTube channel. They have exercise videos that are designed for moms and target all areas of the body, all in 20 minutes or less. Also, please keep in mind that it might be harder and might take longer to get back down close to your pre-pregnancy weight despite your workouts and meal plan. I know it can be frustrating when you want to get back to normal, but be patient. Your body will take time to bounce back.

THINGS THEY FAIL TO TELL YOU DURING PREGNANCY

Chapter 6
My Ultimate Lists and Must Haves

This chapter contains lists for every stage of your pregnancy. I include items and ideas that were personally helpful to me, and some that first-time moms especially might not think of.

During pregnancy:

• Belly band – If you carry low or just feel uncomfortable, this band/sling helps with lumbar support and discomfort.

• Prenatal vitamins – There are regular pills or gummies. Try to take with food so you don't feel any nausea.

- Drink plenty of water.

- Eat healthy – Make sure you are getting plenty of protein, dairy, and veggies.

- Light exercise – Light impact and/or aerobic workouts help throughout pregnancy.

- Pregnancy app – This will become helpful for your partner when they want to keep up-to-date on everything baby and pregnancy related.

- Good quality reliable vehicle.

- Calendar – Either paper or digital, calendars will help you remember appointments when pregnancy brain kicks in.

- Health insurance/short-term disability insurance.

- Good slip-on shoes.

- Wedge pillow – These are great when you need to reduce swollen feet and reposition to help with acid reflux.

- Maternity pillow – This pillow helps with positioning so you can still sleep when you're uncomfortable.

- Maternity clothes – You will need pants, shirts, dresses, bras and underwear.

- Adaptive equipment – For me, this was a reacher, shoe horn, and sock aide to help get dressed. There are YouTube videos that can teach you the best ways to use this type of equipment if you're unfamiliar.

- Pads – You may leak when you sneeze, cough, or laugh toward the end. Be prepared to have gas at any moment that you cannot control.

- An extra outfit in your car for if you have an accident.

Postpartum (0-8 weeks):

• Stool softeners – These will help when you need to poop and can make it less painful.

• Water/water bottle – Increasing fluids is a must, especially if you are breastfeeding.

• Prenatal vitamins – Prenatal vitamins contain more of what you need than regular multivitamins, and are fine to continue taking after the baby is born.

• Lactation pills made by Honest Company – These significantly helped with my breastmilk production and contain natural ingredients. You may not need to take a supplement like this, or you may find that there's another brand that makes a version you prefer.

• Pads/Depends – Don't ruin cute underwear while you are still bleeding during postpartum recovery. Place a pad within the Depends to get more use out of them, as there will be tons of blood. This is a temporary issue, so don't feel bad about it.

• Sitz bath – Use this type of bath (similar to a bidet) to clean up your vaginal/anal area. A sitz bath kit can be purchased at most drugstores.

• Pain relief spray – This is an antiseptic numbing spray and was a personal must have.

• Vaginal ice pack – This can be bought, some hospitals provide it, or you can make your own.

• Squirt bottle – The hospital often provides this and you will want to take it with you every time you use the bathroom to clean your vagina. Don't leave home without it.

• Tons of loose clothing – My favorite items to wear were

maternity dresses, as they were easier to use when breastfeeding and going to the bathroom.

• Circular pillow – It will hurt to sit down, and this will help you shift positions, relieving pain and pressure.

• Premade meals – You will be exhausted with round-the-clock feedings, but you need to eat in order to produce breastmilk. Having premade meals in your fridge/freezer just gives you one less thing to stress about.

• Wet wipes – Regular toilet paper will stick to you since you must use the squirt bottle to clean up every time you use the bathroom.

• A babysitter – A friend, family, whoever you want, so you can rest and get a nap in.

• Disposable dishes/silverware – You will be too tired to do dishes and will already be washing tons of bottles.

• Nursing pads – Prepare to leak milk and show through your shirt if you don't have any.

• Coffee – You should only intake small amounts of caffeine of course, but this will help you stay awake.

• Healthy on-the-go snacks – If you have healthy snacks that are ready to go, you'll be eating better without even thinking about it and getting much-needed energy in the process.

• Accept all help – This includes offers to cook, clean, watch the baby, run errands, and buy/bring you a meal.

Breastfeed Haul:

• Motherlove Nipple Cream – Found at Target, this cream helps with sore or cracked nipples, and is all-natural.

• Boppy – A Boppy is a nursing pillow used to prop the baby.

This will help you find the most comfortable position for you and baby, whether you're breastfeeding or napping on the couch with them in your arms.

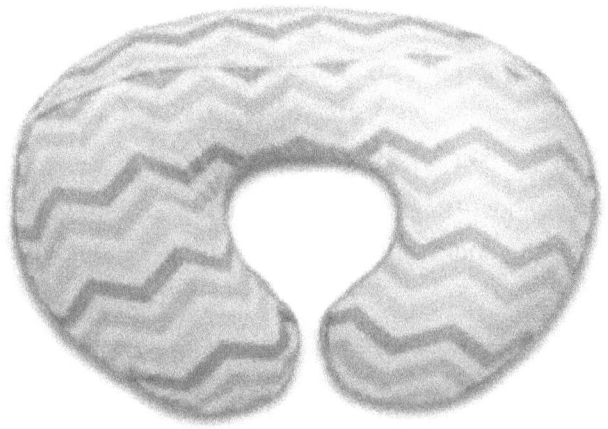

Photo courtesy of Target.com.

• Cover up – This can be a large scarf, a specially designed cover up, or just a blanket to provide privacy while breastfeeding.

• Nipple guard – Some nipples are more sensitive than others; these will help fend off any discomfort.

• Water/water bottle – Whether at home or on the go, drink water to help with production. You will feel dehydrated if you don't.

• Lactation pills/Mother's Milk tea – Both of these help to naturally increase milk supply.

• Extra pumping materials – If you purchase extra materials, you won't have to constantly clean parts before or after you pump.

• Nipple pads/Nursing pads – You place these in your bra to prevent spots when you're leaking.

• Finding a comfortable spot to pump/feed – I was told if you are stressed out or uncomfortable, it can take a toll on your supply. My favorite spot to feed was on the couch, and I only felt comfortable pumping in my car.

Diaper Bag:

• Two or three outfits – Kids easily pee/poo through clothes, so have a couple changes in the diaper bag just in case.

• Diapers

• Wipes

• Changing pad

• Food – You'll want pumped milk, dry formula/supplement, and solid food/snacks when baby is four to six months old.

• Spoon/bowl – You won't need this until the baby is four to six months old.

• Container to hold formula/snacks – I preferred having a container that has three compartments and a lid/spout.

• Water bottle – You'll want a full one if you need to use it for supplement.

• Nursing cover up – Bring this with you if you plan to breastfeed while you are out.

• Toys/teethers – These will be needed around 3+ months.

• Blankets – Receiving blankets, warm blankets (depending on weather), and swaddling blankets are good to have on hand.

• Sunscreen

- Hand sanitizer

- Extra bottles

- Mini soap/laundry detergent – If you are at someone else's home and your baby has a blowout, these will come in handy for a quick cleanup.

- Plastic bags/baggies – You can use these for dirty diapers and dirty clothes.

- Infant meds – Tylenol, Motrin, and gas drops were the ones I usually had with me.

- Bibs, mittens, and hats.

Mom's Hospital Bag:

- Maternity dress – After delivery, you don't want to wear a hospital gown, and it's easier to breastfeed in a maternity dress that has been designed with this in mind.

- Pads/Depends

- Mini Toiletries – If there is a shower in your room at the hospital, you'll want to have your own toiletries with you.

- Bathroom towel – Hospital towels are small and do not absorb like the towels you have at home.

- House shoes/slippers – You'll want to wear these versus the non-skid socks they provide. They will be more cushioned and comfortable.

- Robe – If it's winter time or you get cold easily, a robe will help you stay warm.

- Nursing bra

- Pillow/throw blanket (or two) – These help provide the comfort of home and keep you warm. The hospital blankets are thin. Plus, if your partner or any family members are staying with you, they will appreciate having something nicer than what the hospital offers.

• Heating pad – I used this in triage in-between walking to ease my lower back pain.

• Essential oils – These are great to help you relax.

• Boppy – This was a major lifesaver for me. I it used for not only breastfeeding, but when little guests came to hold the baby as well.

• Clothes for baby, swaddle blanket, and personal items for if you plan on having a photographer come by.

• Things to keep you partner occupied when you are in labor and waiting.

Baby Must-haves, 0-6 Months Old:

• Crib – Convertible to a toddler bed is best and will save you money later on.

• Dresser

• Changing table

• Clothes – You'll want multiple sizes on hand because you'll never know when the baby will outgrow last week's clothes.

• Bibs

• Shects – Have at least three sets for when baby wets through their diaper and clothes.

• Blankets

• Towels/wash cloths

• Humidifier

- Night lights
- Closet clothing organizers
- Blackout curtains
- Baby bottle brush

- A&D ointment with cloths – If you are having a boy and are having him circumcised, this will be useful. A&D ointment is similar to Neosporin for babies to help heal the skin on the penis.

- Small lunch box – If you plan on pumping when returning to work, this will keep milk from spoiling.

- Diaper bag – There are so many options out there. Tons of parents are using backpack versions. I prefer the zip-top utility tote from Thirty-One Gifts. Having pockets to organize your stuff is essential. However, I did transition to a backpack when the baby became more mobile and required fewer things to carry with me.

- Bumbo – This is a molded seat made from low-density foam, which helps with sitting up and feeding time. This seat helps your baby sit supported upright and can be used with a tray to help with feeding and learning to sit up.

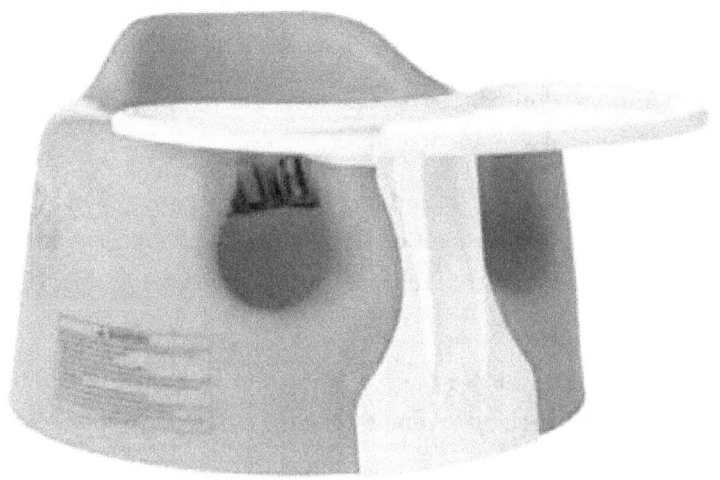

Photo courtesy of Target.com.

• Boppy – These are great for positioning during feedings or when little people are holding the baby.

• Pack 'n Play – This can be used if you are at someone else's house and you don't have a crib.

• 3-in-1 bath – I have a Summer Infant 1-2-3 and love it. It is a big plastic tub that comes with a detachable net to support baby. It's affordable and very sturdy.

• Bottles/spoons/bowls/extra pumping supplies – Dr. Brown's was my favorite bottle.

• Diapers/wipes – I had multiple sizes stocked, and went through five big packs of newborn diapers before needing the next size up.

• CD/sound soother/radio – This will help baby fall asleep, providing them with white noise.

• Portable heater – A safe digital rotating heater that will keep baby warm during cold nights.

- Toys – Teething, tummy time, interactive light up, and developmental toys are a few kinds you'll need early on.
- Bouncer/jumper – Babies love to jump around. Bonus points if it lights up and has music.
- Highchair – My friend is in love with Graco Table2Table Premier Fold 7-in-1 High Chair. She says it's lightweight, folds up easily for storage, and can even turn into a table for growing toddlers.
- Video monitor – I have one (Motorola) that came with an app so I can check up on and talk to my baby, play music for him, check the room temperature, and move the camera from the monitor and my phone.
- Sleepers and nightgowns – Nightgowns are open at the bottom, making it simpler to change diapers at night. It's easier and faster to have a zip-up sleeper versus a snap sleeper.
- Burp cloths – The thick ones are best, not ones that look like a wash cloth. Mine were made by Carter's.
- Foam number/letter squares – These are easier and softer for tummy time if you have wood/tile floors. I like the ones that provide texture and bright colors and can also act as a toy that will hold the baby's attention.
- Travel system – This includes car seat and stroller combined. My favorite is the Baby Trend brand. Very strong, durable, and you can use the stroller without car seat as a base. My husband loved it because the wheels are real tires, with three wheels for easy steering and a smooth ride, four cup holders, amplifier for music for your phone, and a big compartment to carry your stuff. Britex may look cute, but you can only use the stroller with the infant carrier. They will

eventually grow out of this, and now you are out of a stroller again.

Photo courtesy of Walmart.com.

• Convertible car seat – Some parents don't get travel systems. My baby is in a high percentile in height and quickly grew out of his infant car seat. I love Graco's Extend2Fit car seat. The baby can be rear-facing for longer, there were no recalls on the product, it's easy to use, and strong/durable. Plus, my baby liked this car seat better and would no longer cry when placed in it.

• Mirror for the car to spy on baby – You put this on the seat head and it's easier to see baby if they are placed behind the passenger's seat.

• Tummy time gym – Encourage tummy time to strengthen baby's muscles so they won't have any developmental delays. A gym will keep them entertained and engaged.

Photo courtesy of Target.com.

• Glow Seahorse – This is like the 90's glowworm, but also has music. This will be a soothing companion for your baby.

• Mesh crib bumpers – The baby will eventually start putting limbs outside of their crib and will get stuck. These are a soft and safe way to prevent that.

• Rock 'n Play Sleeper – It rocks, provides proprioception, vibration, and an elevated head to help with GERD/acid reflux. This was my ultimate lifesaver. I could not live without this and preferred it over any bassinet. It is very lightweight, transportable with baby in it, and collapses to take with you on the go. I took it everywhere when baby needed to sleep. Recently, they're now made with an automatic rocking feature.

• Baby food maker – You'll need one only if you plan on making your own baby food. This could be a Baby Bullet, Infantino Fresh Squeezed Squeeze Station (which is easily sold out), Little Sprout Squeeze Station (same as Infantino, just a different brand).

Photo courtesy of Target.com.

• Baby food accessories – There are extra pouches you can buy and a spoon attachment to the pouch, which is great if you're not at home.

• Trash can – I used a regular small trash can and it was cheaper than and just as effective as a Diaper Genie in my opinion.

• Baby care kit – This includes: thermometer, nose syringe, hair brush, nail clipper, and syringe for administering medicine.

• Baby wearing device – Some moms like having one of these if they are out and about or even for in the house if they need to be hands-free while doing chores. I have an Ergo Baby and I know many other moms have Ergo Baby or Tula, with or without infant inserts.

Photo courtesy of Target.com.

• Lovie – This is a comfort item that's also used as a toy.

• Bath supplies – Soap, lotion, and anything else you want to use during bath time.

Baby Must-haves, 6-12 Months:

• Books – Start good habits and read every night. The baby will learn that this is a bedtime routine.

• Pull-to-stand toys – The baby will want to practice and get ready for standing and walking. These toys provide them with a safe way to do so.

•Baby gates/play yard – The baby will begin to crawl and walk everywhere. This will prevent them from getting into something that is unsafe.

• Toothbrush – When baby gets teeth, it's time to start brushing to help develop healthy routines and to desensitize their mouth. I started with the finger brush first.

• Baby snacks – Baby biscuit teethers and other snacks that melt in the mouth are good to start with when they transition to solid foods.

• Baby walker toys – These help baby when learning to stand and eventually to walk.

Photo courtesy of Target.com.

• Baby safety gear – This will be anything that locks cabinets, prevents opening doors, and keeps baby from getting into anything unsafe.

• Shoes – Wait until they start walking around to buy these. Before they wear shoes, use socks. They grow out of shoes quickly.

• TV show – Find a TV show that can grasp baby's attention so you can sneak to the bathroom in peace or when you need a non-screaming/crying moment to think. Mickey Mouse Clubhouse is very popular.

• Toy box – There will be tons of toys everywhere. A cute box will help you stay organized. Just throw everything inside, and you're done!

• Play dates – It's great for baby to interact with other kids so they're not used to just you. This will help with social skills.

• Storage boxes – Take clothes that are not being worn anymore out of the closet. Place them in a bin to save if you plan on having more kids, or give them to a mom in need.

• Sippy cups – There are several types to choose from, but most kids tend to like the kind with a straw. These are better for teeth, speech, and language. However, mine preferred the Dr. Brown's that has a spout to begin with.

• Portable booster seat with tray – I have the Summer Infant Deluxe Comfort Folding Booster seat. This was nice when I went out of town or somewhere out that didn't have a highchair to put the baby in. Instead of having your child on your lap and not being able to eat, you can place the baby in the booster, which ties onto the chair with snaps to give you a hands-free meal.

• Shopping cart cover – I got mine at Target. You place the soft material over the cart to soften the base of the cart seat and prevent baby from grabbing onto the handle with their mouth and getting germs. There are many colors available, and some have plush items attached so baby can play. The seat acts not only as a germ barrier, but neutralizes the temperature of the cart seat as well.

• Sensory toys – Think toys that light up, play music, and have different tactile sensations. This type of stimulation helps the baby to learn.

Photo courtesy of Target.com.

Pack and Play

Rock N' Play

Graco Extend2Fit

Tummy Time Activity Gym

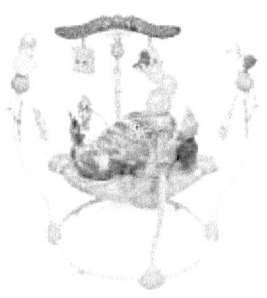
Activity Jumper

Shopping Cart Cover

THINGS THEY FAIL TO TELL YOU DURING PREGNANCY

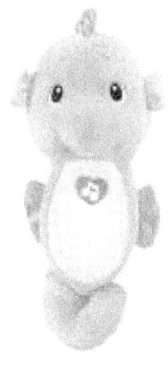
Glow Seahorse

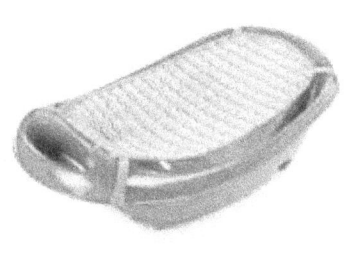
Summer Infant 1-2-3 Bath

Summer Infant Booster Seat

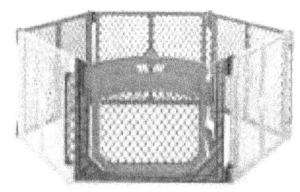
North States Ultimate Play Yard

Sensory Toy

Mesh Crib Liner

Baby Mirror

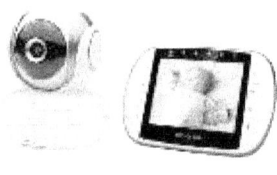

Motorola Baby Monitor

Graco Table2Table High Chair

Newborn Nightgown

Dr. Brown's Sippy Cup

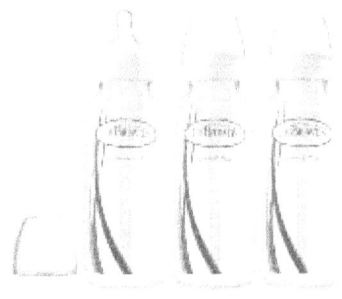

Dr. Brown's Bottles

THINGS THEY FAIL TO TELL YOU DURING PREGNANCY

Chapter 7
How To Save

There are several ways to save on clothes and baby gear. First, let's go for the obvious option, hand-me-downs. Do you know anyone who is done having kids? Because let's face it, they won't want to give anything up until they're finished for good. Sometimes parents will want to clear out some room if they are having a second child and the baby is not the same gender as their first child. If yours is, you could potentially get some items for free or very inexpensively from them. Always try to find anything "free to good home" first to save maximum money. If you are weeks away and running out of time, then turn to purchasing. I used Craigslist and virtual yard sales on Facebook to find anything free to good home. If you are planning a pregnancy, you have time to find anything for free. I waited and got a free crib, changing table, and toddler bed with mattress, which are big expensive items. If you can't find it for free, normally there are options that are very cheap and gently used. Beware: you must be fast and search often, as things go quickly. I even got free formula. I got a lot free formula because my friend's kids only liked one kind, but my kid ate everything.

If you can, and if you want to of course, the best way to save on food/formula is breastfeeding/pumping, making your own food, and with coupons if you'll be using formula. Like I mentioned before, go online and apply for coupons to get five dollars off formula. At my local grocery store (Publix), they offer a baby club. With this baby club, they send coupons for more than just baby items. I received coupons for free rubbing alcohol, hand sanitizer, and money off meat and dairy. Any savings will help.

The second best way to save is at secondhand stores, such as thrift stores (Goodwill and the Salvation Army) and Once Upon A Child. On some days, you can save even more when they have special sales. I know at my thrift store, I found outfits for infants ranging from $0.99 to $2.49. Sometimes these stores even have furniture or toys. A little advice when buying clothes, It's wiser to buy 0-3 month clothes than newborn clothes, unless you have a preemie. The 0-3 month clothes will last you longer overall. Babies sometimes go through several changes a day. Once, my son went through three outfits in one night. My son also grew incredibly fast and remains in a high percentile for height. At nine months, he can wear 12-month clothing, so I buy up in sizes. At Once Upon A Child, I have had friends buy baby bath tubs, clothes, shoes, and toys. Why buy new when a child will grow out of everything so quickly? So, ask around from friends, family, coworkers and Facebook groups on what thrift store they buy from and their locations.

Third, shop at places like Ross, Target, Walmart, or Marshalls. If you can't find it free or at the second-hand stores, this is your next best bet to find good quality clothes, toys, and furniture, depending on the store. At these stores, always check the on sale or clearance rack first. Check for coupons and sales ads, and collect gift cards to save extra money. At Target, they tend to have big baby sales in January and July, especially for car seats. Sometimes you can get the item cheaper if it has any damage. You can also ask if you can buy the floor model for less than the ticketed price. Another way to save is to compare prices online to see who has it cheaper. Keep in mind that some companies like Target offer store-specific promotions like Cartwheel and the REDcard, which sometimes end up being the cheapest and can have free shipping.

I went to a Prego Expo to see new products up close that were not on a shelf and ask questions about the products I was interested in. Not only were you able to see and talk about the products, you could also buy some of them. This expo had everything from car seats and strollers, to smaller items like bottles. As you go around to all the tables they also offer tons of free stuff. To start, they gave me a sippy cup and coupons. As I made my way around the tables, I got two free cans of formula, a rubber ducky, silicone bibs, and a potential door prize. I ended up walking out with a free humidifier. If you're considering going, I would say just do it, you never know what you'll walk away with. All the small items add up, and you could be the one to leave with a big prize like a stroller or car seat!

First, I looked to see what I could get for free until I got too close to my delivery. I asked friends to keep an eye out for anything free or cheap. My friend's next-door neighbor was throwing away a diaper changing table. They were leaving it on the side of the road to be picked up by waste management, so my friend brought me the table the next day. I had friends that shopped regularly tell me when there was a great baby sale. It's hard to buy everything in the span of a few months when baby gear is so expensive. You do not have to have brand new everything unless you have the money and just want to. The only things I really paid a lot for were the car seat and travel system, but please believe I did use gift cards and coupons.

The last way to save money at these big stores is by making a gift registry. After you make a registry to have your last baby shower, you may get duplicates. I returned my duplicates for store credit, and added that to my savings. When you make a registry, many places have a deal where if you don't get everything off your registry and want to finish it out, you can pick whatever else you want that is left. This could be one item or more, and they will give you a percentage off. Make sure you got what you wanted that was left and that it's a big item, like a car seat or travel system. Therefore, it's wise to have more than one registry. Sometimes they give you free stuff and coupons, so you'll also get more than one set of those items if you register at more than one location as well.

Another clever way to save money is to start making DIY projects. If you're not crafty, no worries, there are still simple ways to save a few extra dollars. If you have a changing table, you need a changing pad, right? Wrong; use a bassinet pad. It can be close to half the price and works the same way as a changing pad. I was looking at covers for the bassinet pad and noticed it is the same length as a large pillow. So, instead of buying covers, I used king-sized pillowcases that I already had at home.

I already had an old white painted dresser that I was going to use. I personally didn't care about the color because I just wanted it to be functional. My mother on the other hand wasn't having it, and she came over so she and my husband could sand and paint it to closely match the crib. What really needs to be said here is that it's perfectly fine if your furniture doesn't match. Let's face it, the kid won't notice, won't care, and will grow out of it soon enough. If someone offers you free furniture, just take it and say thank you. My friend had a Winnie the Pooh theme and she had to have everything look a certain way. Everything was dark matching wood, yellow walls, yellow bedding with Pooh. She was even given a free crib, very old but functional, and she gave it to the grandparents and was given a bedroom set that cost over a thousand dollars from Babies "R" Us. If you want, you could go to a thrift store or flea market to buy the pieces and sand them down and stain them yourself for cheaper. Try to not go for a hard theme if you can. I went with Peter Pan and it was gender-neutral and easy to do. There are many ways to do this with pirates, Indians, London, Neverland, mermaids, fairies, an enchanted forest, and ships. If anything you receive is nautical, it will easily fit right in. Don't stress yourself out if it's not completely perfect.

Another big expense can be maternity clothes and nursing bras. I didn't want to go to the mall and pay $40 for one pair of pants. Besides, you will only wear this stuff for second trimester on, and part of postpartum. I went to my thrift store to find pants, and I got name brand pants for around $5 apiece. That was the cheapest I could find, but the only bad thing is you can't always find exactly what you want and must sort through the clothes and try them on. After the thrift stores, try stores like Walmart and Target to find a bigger selection without mall prices. I would first go to the sales and clearance rack to save the most money. Target will sometimes have a deal on their Cartwheel app, which you should take advantage of, even if it's a small percentage off. I also really enjoyed the maternity dresses from Target. I wore them out and about, while in the hospital, and around the house, which made breastfeeding easier.

Finding the right bra can seem like a nightmare; make it a nursing bra, and you have no clue where to go. You can always try the thrift store, hand-me-downs (if possible), Target, and Walmart. I personally am big chested (I'm a DD, to be exact), and I'm picky when it comes to a bra's support and comfort. I know I might have spent a little extra money on this particular item, but the bra I bought, I could even use after breastfeeding. So, when I go bra shopping, I go to Victoria's Secret (you can also try Lane Bryant) because I know what works for me. I got some VSX sport bras that have clips in the front, and they were perfect. I had the support I needed, and it was comfortable and very functional using the front clips for nursing. I also recommend buying a bra extender that attaches to the hook in the back. I bought mine where I purchased my bra, but they are also sold in other stores. I personally am 38 inches around, but when you add extra weight and a pregnant belly, you stretch out even more. You will lose the extra size afterward, and then can use the bra post-baby.

Still on the subject of bras, there is more than one type. You also have pumping bras. Again, the cheapest option is a hand-me-down or thrift store purchase. I have seen them sold online and in-store, but have no clue on exactly what size to get, and for some reason they're always out of the larger sizes. I find this weird to have more smalls when not everyone is tiny. I thought up and made my own, and will walk you through how to make one yourself as well in the next chapter. This can be even cheaper than buying at a thrift store, because more than likely you already have the design components in your dresser.

THINGS THEY FAIL TO TELL YOU DURING PREGNANCY

Chapter 8
DIY (Do It Yourself)

DIY (Do It Yourself) projects can make things cheaper and provide items that are sometimes difficult or impossible to purchase. This final chapter is made up of things I did for myself with a little help from the "What's Up Moms" channel on YouTube. These three moms are the queens of DIY. They show you in their videos how to make delicious and healthy food (including lactation cookies), how to make maternity pants, how to make things for the home (including nursery), and how to recover from afterbirth. I am so glad that I found this channel! I have done DIYs provided by Brooke, cooked healthy recipes from Meg, and had some great laughs from the parody videos by Elle. I swear to everyone I meet that they have the best parenting channel, and I'm inspired by them to be the best mom I can be.

Vaginal Ice Pack

What you will need:

- Diapers

- Medical tape (clear or cloth)

- Ice

- Knife/scissors

I was advised by a nurse how to make these, since this is what was given to me at the hospital. First, you will take the diaper and where it catches the pee, you will make a slit horizontally along the diaper. Then add ice and use medical tape to close it (scotch tape will not be strong enough).

Maternity Pants

What you will need:

- Pants/shorts

- Scissors

- Sewing kit (needle and thread)

- Elastic

- Straight pins

First, start cutting at the top of the waistband along the side seam and cut out the whole pocket. Next, cut the elastic to twice the amount that you had cut off from the pants to fill up the gap. Use straight pins to help line elastic and to keep in place for sewing. After sewing, trim off excess elastic material. There are other ways to do maternity pants, but Brooke from "What's Up Moms" did it the simplest.

<u>Pumping Bra</u>

What you will need:

- Old or new sports bra (racerback with no padding that provides tight support)
- Sharpie
- Pump attachment
- Scissors

First, put on the bra and put the part of pump that goes over the nipple on. Do not have the part of the pump where it connects to where the tube goes for suctioning. Then with the cover of the pump off, see where it lines up with your nipple and use the Sharpie where the inside of the lines goes for the pump. Lastly, cut out the circles you have made when the bra is off. I would wear this bra, then place my "nursing bra" (Victoria's Secret VSX sports bra with front clip) over it and when I needed to pump I unclipped the front and pulled it down. I then placed on my pumping attachments through the holes and it would hold in place while pumping making this experience hands free. A little tip is to place a nursing pad inside the nursing bra and not the pump bra for maximum comfort. Unless you're at home, don't wear the pump bra without the nursing bra in case of leaking and for comfort.

<u>Soothing Maternity Pads Two Ways</u>

What you will need:

- Big oversized pad (with or without wings, your preference)

- Tucks (or pads soaked in witch hazel)
  - Aloe

This is simple. Take the Tucks or soaked pads and place it on top of pad, but use it like soft cheese, and spread it out over entire pad. Before pulling up your pants, use pain relief spray and you are ready to go.

For the second option, take the witch hazel and pour onto pad, then apply aloe and freeze. This is closer to an ice pack feel, but still soothing. I would only wear this if you are staying at home. The above DIY is what I constantly did, and was easier to change if I was out of the house. They had an easy clean-up and application.

<u>Tips for Making Homemade Baby Food</u>

What you will need:

- Fresh or frozen food
- Way to steam food (fruits and veggies)
- Peeler (so there is no skin on the food)
- Food processor/blender
- Pouches/container
- Squeeze station (if using pouches)
- High grade/quality strainer (for very pureed foods)

For recipes, you can check mom blogs, get recipes from friends, "What's Up Moms," and general searches online. Not going to lie, I failed at first. I had forgotten to peel and steam my fruits and didn't have a strainer to make my food puree. It came out a bit chunky, and baby was having a difficult time eating it. Use "What's Up Moms" for a step-by-step video see what they used, and how they made and stored food. The first foods your baby will eat are one-food recipes to rule out any food allergies. At first, my son would develop a rash on his forehead on one temple. Our pediatrician said it was okay, as long as he was breathing and not having worsening adverse reactions. He eventually stopped developing a rash after eating pureed bananas. When you have given them several other foods, then you can go to stage two and start mixing and matching fruits and vegetables. My favorite was to do a fruit-type cocktail. However, my kid has always been a great eater and has never refused any meal. Another favorite I would do would make a smoothie that I had found from "What's Up Moms." The recipe consisted of 1 cup of orange juice, 1 peeled banana (fresh or frozen), 1 cup of mixed frozen fruit, ½ cup nonfat Greek yogurt, handful of baby spinach and optional 2-3 teaspoon of chia seeds. I liked all the ingredients and that the entire family could have this together.

<u>Organizing Clothing Spacers</u>

What you will need:

- Shower curtain hangers (white or clear)
- Scissors (optional)
- Sharpie
- Colored tape (washi tape)

First, you will take the round curtain hangers and cover them with tape. You can either cut strips of tape or wrap the tape fully around the hanger. Use the Sharpie to label the sized clothing: newborn, 0-3 months, 3 months, 3-6 months, 6 months, 6-9 months, 9 months, 9-12 months, 12 months, 12-18 months, 18 months, 18-24 months, and 24 months. After these sizes, it will go 2T, 3T, and 4T. This was very helpful when hanging up clothes after doing laundry. Plus, you can see and use what fits currently. It also makes easier to take smaller clothing away to store after it no longer fits. This keeps baby's closet organized and makes dressing your baby fast and easy.

Chapter 9
Man's Survival Guide

Your partner is pregnant. Every man in this place wonders, "What do I do?" From my husband's perspective, not much until the baby arrives. The advice in this chapter is what my husband would tell other dads to-be, and it's what he found to be helpful to him while I was pregnant. Take what you want from his experience and tips.

First, get involved by going to the doctor's appointments to learn what's going on with mom and baby. Even though he felt a certain degree of disconnection to his wife and baby, this helped him feel more connected in a different way. Another way to see how the baby is developing and what your partner might be experiencing is by downloading a pregnancy app. Try to look at it for the first time together. This makes it new for the both of you, and will be a nice bonding and learning experience.

Another important topic is sex. Everyone is different in how much/often they want sex. All the man needs to know is that it is perfectly safe to have sex throughout the entire pregnancy. Every man seems to think that their penis is going to hit the uterus and/or hit the baby. Don't worry, there's no chance in that happening. Sex will be different when the belly is huge, so all you need to do is find different positions that you're both comfortable with. Postpartum is a whole different story. You need to give your partner anywhere between six to eight weeks of rest, from a medical standpoint. However, if she needs more time, give it to her because it's scary for her. She will be sore and bleeding for a long time, will feel unattractive, and it will hurt at first for her. Just be patient, and she'll let you know when she's ready.

Seeing the sonogram and feeling the baby's first kick is when the reality sets in for most dads. If your partner says she feels a kick and you can't, this is normal. Just be patient, you'll eventually feel it, too. Even though you're preparing for a baby, don't forget about your partner, and spend as much quality time as you can together; this will help keep her sane. Many men foresee a pregnancy like the ones seen in movies and TV shows. Remember, the entertainment industry is meant to entertain you. My husband was waiting for weird cravings, late-night runs to the store, and the moment during labor when I would squeeze his hand so tightly, I'd break it. None of these things happened. Every woman is different, so don't stereotype her;

you'll only annoy her.

If you're planning on moving, do it as soon as possible. This will get harder for your partner to do the closer to delivery she is. When we were looking to move, we wanted extra space, but only if it fit in the budget. We were lucky and got a great deal on a rental that had extra rooms. Part of the ultimate man survival guide (in my husband's opinion) is having your own space, such as a man cave of some sort. It can be in a spare room, garage, or even a shed. He liked that he could escape for a while and have his own stuff. Coming from a wife's point of view, he had to have it. My husband likes his games and his shows, and before this, his area was the living room. There was nowhere to entertain guests, and the noise level was an issue. It was nice that he could have his own room to put all his stuff where he wanted, and when it got too noisy, he could easily fix it by shutting the door. This makes us both happy, and keeps us both sane.

Before baby, especially if you are not moving, get the nursery done. "Done" means having everything out of the box and put together. Sometimes a baby can come early, and you don't want to come home and have to put everything together all at once and stress out about it. Not only will your partner be in panic mode and feel stressed, you will have to hear her complain the entire time you're putting it together. Another thing you'll need to do is install the car seat early and learn how to use it. If you decide to get an Infant car seat, it's best to have at least two bases, so you have one to put in each car. If you get the convertible car seat, get two; one for each vehicle. This will be a less of a headache in the end. I had to convince my husband that each car should have its own car seat, and I'll tell you why. A convertible car seat is big and bulky and takes strength to tighten the belt to make sure it's secure. This gets tiring if you're constantly changing them out. It's worth the time and money to have the flexibility to get up and go, especially since parents with children are often running late. The last thing to do before baby arrives is to make sure the majority of what is needed, like the diaper bag and the hospital bag, is already in the car.

Now that everything is prepped, your partner is ready to go to the hospital. During this labor process, your partner will be in too much pain and will need help. Remember, before you head out, there are three things that need to be done in this process. First, after you have timed the contractions to five minutes apart lasting no less than a minute each for about 30 minutes or more, call the doctor's office, even if it's after-hours. The number will route you to who you need to speak with to get a hold of the on-call doctor. The doctor will be paged, and you'll get a call back. Tell them about the contractions, like how long the contraction is lasting and how far apart they are. From there, the doctor will decide whether to admit you or if you should wait a bit longer. If they say to come on in, they will pre-admit you, making it easier to get back into triage. If you don't call the doctor first and go to the hospital and they don't think you're ready to be admitted, they'll send you home. This five-minute phone call could save you tons a time and potentially an additional car ride. The second they give you the green light to come in, place the rest of your things in the car and head to the hospital. As a warning, try not to jerk the car by speeding it up; this makes the contractions feel worse. Lastly, call any loved ones you'd like before leaving, and tell them that you are on your way to the hospital. Let them know whether you want them at the hospital or not. If you don't tell them not to come, chances are, they'll likely show up.

Now that you're settled in the labor and delivery room, you will eventually get hungry, but your partner can't eat or drink.

Go grab something to eat in the hospital or nearby. Ask hospital staff if they like the food there and what they order. More than likely, they'll tell you what to steer clear from. If you're going stir crazy, go grab something somewhere close by and have a change of scenery, because all you've got to look at when you return are four walls with no windows. During this time, be patient and ready for everything. Every labor is different and you never know how long you'll be in that room or if you will be transferred to surgery if an emergency C-section is needed. Expect your partner to be dehydrated since she is not allowed food or liquids now, but she can have ice chips. This logic may seem absurd, but this is to prevent vomiting. The ice chips take time to melt down and can slowly hydrate your partner. If you were to hand her a cup of water, she'd down it in no time, increasing chances of vomiting.

In-between feeding your partner ice chips, if the labor is going slowly, they usually have a TV, internet, and games (not console gaming). To pass time, my husband brought his own stuff, since he knew he would be with me overnight. His bag consisted of clothes, a blanket, a light jacket, a pillow, and gadgets such as his tablet to keep himself entertained. He kept his jacket and tablet into labor and delivery, and the rest he brought up after we moved into a regular non-birthing room. Both of our moms were in the labor and delivery room, switching off caretaking shifts with my husband, so he could squeeze in a nap when it was necessary. Without these extra hands, he would have been up during the entire labor process, which ended up being 26 hours total.

When the baby starts to come, your partner will be exhausted and will need help during the pushing phase. You may need to help her bend forward or hold up her legs. This is straining and exhausting, which is another reason why it's nice to have extra help. When the baby comes out, cut the cord. This is a nice bonding experience with your baby. No need to worry, the doctor will clamp the cord twice and where tell you where to cut, and no, there will be no blood expelling out of it. Have your picture taken with the baby while your partner is being stitched up. If you have the new grandmas with you, there will be tons of pictures. Your partner will thank you for this later since she will be exhausted and in no position to take them herself.

During your stay at the hospital, the father will receive a daily food voucher. The hospital will tell you how much food the voucher allows and how to get them during hospital orientation. My husband just ate half of what I ordered, because I couldn't eat much. If you have visitors, they tend to bring you food and gifts for the baby. There isn't tons of space, but there is a pull-out couch to sleep on. My husband is thin and shared my hospital bed with me, which is also an option if you feel comfortable doing so. If your partner expects to breastfeed, then there's not a ton you can do besides change diapers. Husbands tend to get more sleep than wives, so let her get a few naps if possible.

Now that it's time to go home, the reality sets in. This is scary for both new mom and dad. There is no right or wrong way of doing things because you don't have a routine yet, and that's okay. Within the first week of being home, you'll see the pediatrician, and there are several more visits soon after that. Try to get ready earlier than you usually would to be there on time. You are used to rushing your partner out the door, and now there is another person added to the mix. It will take more time to get ready, so prep anything you can and do things to help you get out the door sooner. If possible, you'll need to take off no less than one week from work.

Your partner will need some help, whether it's diaper changes, making meals, or housework. You'll also need to make sure she stays awake when she has the baby. Several times, my husband has tapped my shoulder or called out my name to wake me up, because breastfeeding will wear you down. He was worried at first about diaper changes and was afraid of vomiting. He says what helps him is breathing through his mouth and not looking at it as much. At first it doesn't smell much. What's worse than the smell is the intense blowouts, which no one can prepare you for. A blowout is when poop is everywhere, even outside the diaper. Just jump in with taking care of the child during diaper changes, feeding if she pumps or if it's supplement, bathing, and learn to make bottles if you use formula. Just be involved with mom and baby, because the first few weeks fly by and before you know it the baby is about to have their first birthday.

When it comes to parenting, just take your time, ask for help, and don't be too hard on yourself. This will be overwhelming for both you and your partner. If the baby is crying even though they just had feeding time, don't just hand the baby back in defeat. Try to see what you can do to soothe the baby, because you will watch your child by yourself, whether your partner is out shopping or just showering. Start learning your baby's routine once they form a consistent one. But remember, routines can change at the drop of a hat, and that's okay; just roll with it. The best advice is to be patient, persistent, and present. What my husband said helped was spending quality family time together, whether it was going to the park or out to breakfast. The more you're in tune with your family, the more you know about each person. You'll be able to distinguish between hungry cries and tired cries. My husband's hardest time is when he feels like the baby prefers mom over him. Persist through, because there will be a time where the baby will want you more over mom.

Lastly, be observant, especially if you have animals, to see how the animals interact with the baby. Even though the animal may have great intentions and want to be loved on and played with, they sometimes are unaware of their size, claws, and teeth. Always be present and if they're nearby, try not to have your eyes on the screen as much. Also keep in mind how your animals behave by looking at body language; who knows, they may or may not be jealous. You may have to give them extra time when baby is sleeping to help promote good behaviors.

All in all, do your best and be present in the moment. It's easy to become disconnected and drift away, because at times you can feel left out from the bond the mom shares with the new baby. Jump in and help with the baby, don't wait for her to ask, notice what needs to be tended to it even if it's one task a day. Take opportunities to capture moments of her with the baby. This will be a perfect Mother's Day gift, so keep this idea in the back of your mind, because let's face it, she's the one taking the pictures. Learn your child's routines for sleeping, eating, and what helps to soothe them. You need to be able to care for your child when mom is away or out buying groceries.

THINGS THEY FAIL TO TELL YOU DURING PREGNANCY

Chapter 10
Mom Life

You just get home from the hospital, and now your world has changed. There are late-night feedings, cries that wake you from a light sleep, and endless diaper and clothing changes. You feel like it is continuously eat, sleep, change, poop, and repeat for a while. If you plan on breastfeeding, at times you will feel like a nursing milk cow. It can make you feel unattractive, and you might not want your partner to mess with your boobs. Let's face it, if he messes with them, there's possible milk leakage that can happen. I have tried to reposition them and have squirted my own face. It also takes a while to get used to from a positioning standpoint. Then if you choose to pump, there's another whole new thing to get used to. At first, you typically will hold the pumps doing nothing for 15 minutes, feeling bored and guilty for not accomplishing a task. Then you should also find a place where you feel comfortable to pump, especially when company is visiting you and the baby.

Next are doctor's appointments, not only for you at six to eight weeks, but for baby, too. The baby will have several appointments in the beginning, then they start to spread out a bit as time moves on. Learning how early to leave to make appointments in time, or even going to the store can be a challenge. I would go and grab only the few things that I absolutely needed. I would put the baby carrier inside the cart so I knew the baby would be safe, and put stuff up top or around the carrier. I would take the baby in the infant carrier to my favorite restaurant and ask for the infant slings, because it's much safer than using a chair. I had no clue this infant sling existed until the staff showed me how to use it. Infant slings are at restaurants and normally the host or waiter will ask if you would like to use one. I have seen two different types. One goes on top of the chair to extend the base of the chair to places the infant car seat can be placed on. The second one is freestanding—imagine a TV tray without the hard top, but instead there's a sling. This also provides a big base of support for the car seat and can be placed next to you.

Enjoy showering and washing your hair now while they sleep tons at first. When they get a little older, you may live on dry shampoo and putting your hair up in a messy bun. You may be in a hurry and find either mismatched clothes or sometimes yesterday's outfit because you are running around crazy. It might be rare if you wear makeup and jewelry, and that's okay. No one will notice you as much, they'll notice the baby more. When they sleep, you have a few choices: showering, napping, eating, cleaning, working, phone calls, or time with your partner or yourself. Don't guilt yourself for choosing what you want to do versus what you probably should have done. Things can wait; they're not going anywhere. If you decide to nap over doing dishes, don't worry; they won't grow legs and walk away.

If you choose to return to work, things can get challenging. Tons of new moms struggle with this. First, what are your hours and is there any flexibility? Fortunately, I could go in early and be home a bit after lunch time. This gave me several hours with my baby compared to a couple of hours, and worked well for me. I could have the flexibility to spend more time with my baby, but I also was very tired all the time because I was working and being a mom. I was lucky that my husband was a full-time daddy working part-time on the weekend and gave a dedicated family day. In most cases, both parents must go back to work and either you put your kid in daycare, or you have family watch them if you can. I had friends who had the flexibility to go into work early, but their family didn't want to get up that early to watch the baby. I know this can suck and make you feel guilty because you feel like you are cheated out of time with your family. It's okay; you're doing what's best for your family.

Personally, I got the opportunity of experiencing both sides of working up until my accident, and then was home recovering. I enjoyed working because I got a bit of a break and I felt that I cherished my time so much more when I got home. I would tell my husband I was good and wanted to let him have some of his own "me time" to escape. Now that I have no break and no other adult interaction (because with my injury I now can't drive and am stuck at home), I go stir crazy. I am a very active person, even if it's just running errands, and being stuck at home is no cakewalk. I think it's harder to stay home and try to keep everything together. Let's face it, you can only tolerate so much crying and the baby grabbing on you before you want to scream.

If you do get to the point of screaming, it's okay; we've all been there and you're not a bad mom, you're human. My best advice is just to walk away and tell your partner to take over. It's normal to feel frustrated, even if you think it's stupid. I would be annoyed when I fed the baby and it took forever due to the baby being distracted. My husband would be in the room and all the baby wanted to do was stare at hubby, so I got up and had hubby finish the feeding.

Going out is not as easy as it used to be. There might be a girl's night out or a potential date night with your partner, and unless you can get a sitter, you're not going out. This can be hard in different ways. If you go you may feel guilty that you left your baby behind. Most moms don't want to leave them for a while, even if just for a few hours, when they're a newborn. Then there's the situation where you couldn't get a sitter, so once again, you'll be staying in for the night. I found a great alternative was to have friends or family come to my house because it was easier to be in charge of my surroundings. You can order take out, have a glass of wine, and have the comfort of your own home. If you plan on company coming when you normally put the baby to bed, you can have some uninterrupted time.

Having time for yourself and your partner will not happen very often. Still, make time for yourself and each other, whether it's going out for a date or a night in on the couch. From the time I wake, I am with the baby until he goes to sleep. This can be challenging because there are never enough hours in the day. Try to prioritize what you need to do, whether it's doing chores or having some much-needed alone time. I can do some chores when the baby is up when he's occupied or if I'm willing to let him cry for a few minutes. Find what works best for you, but make sure you get time for you, even if it's soaking in a tub with peace and quiet.

Be prepared for the messiness that comes with having children. Expect to be peed on, vomited on, a blowout poopy diaper that is everywhere, drool, food/formula on them and you, sticky hands, and dirty clothes. All this has happened, and you will survive. All you can do is be as prepared as you can if you are out, and know that it all can be washed away with a bath, new diaper, and clothes. Once the baby peed through his diaper onto me and we ended up changing our clothes a total of five times between the two of us in one night. Another time, I was trying to feed him before work and he vomited all over my shirt. Just grab a wash cloth, wipe off your body, and grab another shirt. For the blowout poopy diaper, you are never prepared mentally for this. These are much easier to handle if they happen at home. For those experiencing this in public, you may also want to carry some extra clothes in your car for yourself along with having extra baby clothes. My baby pooped while in a sleeper outfit, so the majority was contained. However, the poop managed to come out of the diaper and leaked onto the blanket he was on. This is when you just get off as much poop as you can and place them in the bathtub. This might have been the first, but was certainly not the last blowout.

This might sound odd, but at times it can be difficult and exhausting to entertain your baby. This is why play dates can be amazing for both mom and baby. When they are little and cannot really move while doing tummy time, take time to do floor stretches for yourself. When they get older and become mobile by rolling, crawling, and walking is when it becomes exhausting. A baby's attention span does not last very long. Have toys that will grab their attention. These are normally sensory toys. To keep things fresh so they don't get bored so easily, change out toys here and there, rotating them unless they have a favorite. Always keep the favorite available. When they're crawling and walking around is when you will appreciate having a big play yard up. You'll want one with a door, as it will be easier for you. I would place toys in there and sometimes a favorite show on in the background, so I could run and get ready or even to use the bathroom in peace. Most of the time my baby hates to be alone and I seem to be sitting in the cage playing with him to keep him occupied. The bright side is, you're wearing out the baby's energy and keeping them from getting into whatever you don't want their hands on.

You will start taking so many pictures and videos of the baby, that you'll have more pictures of them now than of the pet you've had for the past five years. Capture these moments not only for nostalgia, but also because they can make awesome gifts for the holidays. Be careful of how much you talk about or shove your baby's picture in your friends' or coworkers' faces. Some people don't mind hearing the funny story about your baby, but some might not care or be thrilled about it. Don't take it personally, just learn who you can gush as much as you want to (with a limit, of course) to keep friends near you rather than pushing them away.

You may have read several books and are trying to be the ultimate best mom. You may be doing well at keeping up your night routine of reading. Don't beat yourself up when you either forget, are too tired, or had a change in plans. I found it harder to maintain a routine when friends and family were around at bedtime. If you were tired and forgot, don't just give up, you can try again the next night and the night after that. Life doesn't go perfectly planned like how you made it seem on paper, be flexible and know it is okay for things to go wrong. For other routines, try to keep a visual aid like a calendar for motivation and accountability. Don't be upset if you are not the mom you envisioned yourself to be. At least having the best intentions means that you care and want the best for your family. Things can get overwhelming pretty quickly, and it can take a while to have a routine that sticks, especially when the baby constantly changes up their routine.

Welcome to new mom guilt; it sucks and it's hard to shake off. You will feel guilty of things that are out of your control and things you later will finally consider to be small stuff. I would feel guilty to sleep in while my husband was caring for our child. You feel guilty about going out and recharging yourself. You'll feel guilty leaving them with a sitter. It's a never-ending cycle. You always feel like you never do enough. Believe it or not, they won't remember any of this, so try not to stress out over it. But remember, the world does not hang only on your shoulders, let others help you. Have your partner watch their own kid. I know I can be a control freak and I will see my husband take care of the kid but not the way I do it. It will be fine, let them care for the kid in their own way and let them figure out what works for them. From the beginning, if you make it out that you will do everything, that will be what is expected of you. Don't start this trend, because it will later end in fights and disagreements. I had my husband do everything I did: diaper changes, feedings, changing clothes, nighttime routine, bathing, and play time. Believe it or not, we all survived. Just try not to get stuck in the past. You know, back in the day when the entire house was cleaned by you, a hot meal was on the table that was prepared by you, your makeup was perfect, and your best clothes and jewelry were on. I say look to the future and do things based on what you see, but not entirely by yourself—have your partner step up and help. Remember, they don't babysit their own children, they raise and parent them too, just like you.

Lastly, persevere on through the tough times and enjoy every memory being made. They're only babies once, and before you know it, they'll be graduating from school and you'll wonder where the time went. Be as present as you can and don't take things for granted. Don't beat yourself up if you wanted to stay home and had to work, the baby won't remember it—only you will. Do the best that you can with what you've got to work with. A child will always hold onto your warmth, love, and patience more than everything. So, laugh with them, cry with them, and show them how much you love them and get all the kisses that you can before they tell you to stop because they think they're too grown up. And be the mom you want to be, not what the TV, family, friends, or the world tells you to be.

Summary/ Final Thoughts

The biggest saying I had to repeat since becoming a mom was "I'm not perfect." Becoming a parent can be a stressful transition. You have this idea in your head from the beginning of what you want to do and what type of parent you will be. That went out the window for me. I did things that fit into my life and my daily routines rather than what I thought I should have done, what other moms did, or what I thought society expected me to do. When I started to do what made my life easier, the less stress I had. With this being said, don't put your beliefs onto other moms and don't judge them for what they do. My best friend admired that I had become the laid-back mom. She admitted as much as she wishes she could be laid-back she is not that type, which is fine. She did appreciate that I never judged her for the choices in parenting style and I continued to provide her support and suggestions if needed. There's more than one way of parenting, and that's fine. Try not to lose yourself, partner, family, and friends. Always make time for people, including yourself; you'll thank yourself later. Learn that if you forget to brush their teeth before bed, give them sweets, give them fast food because life gets hectic, it's okay; the kid is still alive. Don't overdo it to strive for perfection, strive for your normal and go on from there.

Learn what works for you. Some moms will tell you what they have or used and what has worked for them. If you are at your wits end, then sure, try anything. But it's okay if their advice doesn't pan out. Take what they said and modify to make it work better for you. Be sure to have mom friends, as they're very important. I had an experienced mom of two (going on three) babies send me a video on Facebook (she's out of state, husband is in the military) on how to put a baby on/off your back using an Ergo Baby Carrier. She filmed herself doing this, since she didn't like the videos on YouTube. It's also nice to have mom friends to be able to socialize your baby and yourself amongst friends. Having mom friends gives you someone you can relate your stress and guilt to. I have weekly conversations with my friend and we talk out our "bad mom moments." This is a great support system so you don't feel alone in your day-to-day life struggles of being a new mom. You will be amazed by having these conversations. My friend thought I did more for my baby than she did and vice versa. This makes you feel more human and it gives you a good laugh at the end. By the end of the phone call you have lifted each other up and feel so much better about yourself.

Lastly, my biggest thing I cannot stress enough is to be yourself. Do what makes you happy, do what makes your life easier, and keeping doing it. Some people (more so family) will bombard you on what they think you should do and how you should do it. I'm talking family members or friends who take control and you feel like they're telling you what to do and how to raise this baby. You can listen to their ideas, but you don't have to act upon them. This can make you stressed out during pregnancy and postpartum. Listen to your gut, your intuition. I have taken some advice and was very thankful for it, like with sleep training. Due to taking my mother-in-law's advice, my baby has been in the crib sleeping through the night since he was two months old. But it was my choice to take her advice. If you constantly try to please others to make them happy or make things easier for you, you are the one who suffers. Think about yourself, your family, and your mental health. There are times I wished I didn't do something or go somewhere. Now, if I don't want to do something or go somewhere, I won't. I think how this will affect the baby's routine and mine, and I ask myself how much sleep will I lose over this. Remember, you're not alone, ask for help, ask for guidance if needed, and don't take everything upon yourself. Besides, you didn't make this baby alone, and the saying is true that it takes a village to raise a child.

About The Author

Ashley Shayne Pierce is mom to a baby boy named Connor. Before having Connor, she obtained an Associates of Science degree in Occupational Therapy Assistant from Keiser University in Tampa, Florida. In school, she learned different areas of practice, including pediatrics. She learned sensory techniques and stages of independence for children performing ADLs (activities of daily living). Having a child, Ashley was able to include handling techniques and applying what she had learned from school she transferred that into her parenting into motherhood.

Ashley has also taken classes in American Sign Language from a local community college. She has learned and watched many YouTube videos from the channel "What's Up Moms" for inspiration to be the best mom she could be.

After being involved in a car accident which resulted in losing half her kneecap and forced her to wear a straight leg brace for five months, Ashley had to learn to do things differently to care for her son. This made Ashley think outside the box to provide care to her son while being injured. This experience helped her grow as a mom and as a clinician by learning and teaching others how things can be done differently. Ashley and her husband Andrew reside in Tampa, Florida, where they have lived together since 2006.

Sources

"What's Up Moms" YouTube Channel:
www.youtube.com/channel/UCMfXv2enRXepxG92VoxfrEg